THE DOWNTON ERA

GREAT HOUSES, CHURCHILLS, AND MITFORDS

THE DOWNTON ERA

GREAT HOUSES, CHURCHILLS, AND MITFORDS

NANCY C. PARRISH

Matador
9 Priory Business Park,
Wistow Road, Kibworth Beauchamp,
Leicestershire, LE8 0RX
Tel: 0116 279 2299
Email: books@troubador.co.uk
Web: www.troubador.co.uk/matador
Twitter: @matadorbooks

ISBN 9781838592103

British Library Cataloguing in Publication Data.
A catalogue record for this book is available from the British Library.

Typeset in 11pt Caslon Pro by Troubador Publishing Ltd, Leicester, UK

Matador is an imprint of Troubador Publishing Ltd

For Ei

CONTENTS

AMERICA'S
GUILTY PLEASURE

On a Saturday in May 2018, twenty-nine million Americans set their alarm clocks for 4 a.m., poured Bloody Marys or mimosas, and settled in to watch a seismic shift in British history – an American divorcée becoming a Royal without creating a constitutional crisis. Another American divorcée, Wallis Simpson, did the same in 1936; but her fiancé had to give up his throne and accept banishment from the country he literally was born to rule.

Meghan Markel, a divorced American woman, was marrying Prince Harry Windsor, the man fifth in line to the throne of the United Kingdom. Certainly, the beauty of the bride and the reputation of the now-tamed Prince factored in the blanket network coverage; and, undeniably, the country thirsted for some pleasant news. But still, royals in Thailand, Brunei, and Saudi Arabia have more wealth and power than the English royals. European nobles in Monaco, Sweden, and the Netherlands have titles as ancient and dress as elegant. So, what made this wedding a transatlantic phenomenon?

I suggest one explanation is found by tracing the arc of the British aristocracy through the lives of their family seats and castles – the physical bricks and mortar of privilege and decline. History is generous in offering two intertwined families – the Churchills and the Mitfords – to illustrate this arc. From the 1700s to the 1900s, this titled group lavished a fantastic wealth, took paramours among their friends and families, and passed the reins of political power to their heirs like a birthright. They marched across the continents of the earth, leaving behind them a map recolored in the red of the British Empire. They lived life on a high wire where family rifts played out in the papers and across nations; where politics were so personal that families ruptured over fascism and socialism; where commitments flamed so passionately that sisters would willingly condemn a sibling to prison for holding an opposing view. They dominated the government during peacetime and led armies in the wars their country chose to wage. Their lifestyles achieved the level of artistry.

Yet there were dark seeds sown in this privilege. Regardless of the artistic ideal their country houses and castles may have embodied, those elegant, massive structures walled the nobles away from the economy and morality of the country they governed and sent into battle. It was within these walls –in this rarefied atmosphere–that the aristocracy first flourished and then ultimately declined. As the nineteenth century turned into the twentieth, the loosening of their commanding grip revealed history unfolding like tragedy.

As Americans, we pride ourselves on our republican separation from the British monarchy; yet we have never lost our fascination with the British aristocracy. The television audience generated by the Windsor-Markel wedding is not a new phenomenon by any means. American viewership of *Downton Abbey*, tracing the spiraling fortunes of the fictitious Grantham family-seat, was measured in the multi-millions. American hotels now offer elegant high teas; American tour companies design *Stay-In-A-British-Castle* lodgings. Perhaps the most striking example of our American passion traces back to the Gilded Age where one newspaper magnate, whose means matched his fascination, just went out and *bought* a castle.

CHAPTER 1

———————————

"WANT BUY CASTLE
IN ENGLAND"

On a hot California day in 1925, newspaper magnate William Randolph Hearst drove to his construction project overlooking a bay midway between San Francisco and Los Angeles. His mountainous 250,000-acre ranch was called *Rancho Piedra Blanca* – White Stone Ranch – and here, as a boy and a young man, Hearst had loved to camp, hike, and savor the glorious view down to the curving peninsula protecting the bay below. However, at age 56, Hearst confided in architect Julia Morgan, "I get tired of going up there and camping in tents. I'm getting a little too old for that. I'd like to get something that would be a little more comfortable." So, in 1919 Morgan began designing something "a little more comfortable" that also met Hearst's other more extraordinary specifications.

Hearst was delighted with the progress on the project. Nevertheless, on this particular day, August 13, 1925, he also took a few moments to send a cable to London. The recipient of the cable was Alice Head, editor of Hearst's three-year-old British version of *Good Housekeeping*. She read the message multiple times to make sure she had not imagined it:

WANT BUY CASTLE IN ENGLAND PLEASE FIND WHICH ONES AVAILABLE STDONATS [sic] PERHAPS SATISFACTORY AT PROPER

1

PRICE BUT PRICE QUOTED SEEMS VERY HIGH SEE IF YOU CAN GET RIGHT PRICE ON STDONATS OR ANY OTHER EQUALLY GOOD

HEARST

The brief cable was stunning: in under forty words Hearst had authorized Head to see about the purchase of any English castle of good quality at an acceptable price. The request was probably unique in the history of the world; and, as a personal order from her American boss, it sent a dazed Head scurrying to turn her hand to the task.

Any observer standing beside Hearst at that moment would have been equally startled; because on this day when Hearst authorized the purchase of an English castle, he was overseeing the construction site of what would become the spectacular Hearst Castle. He fondly referred to his castle overlooking San Simeon Bay as "the ranch," but he formally named it *La Cuesta Encantada,* The Enchanted Hill. Its construction—which cost over half a billion dollars in current value—would rival those of any British great house and take thirty years to complete.

La Cuesta Encantada became a sprawling complex containing 165 rooms, 127 acres of gardens, tennis courts, swimming pools, and even an airfield. Hearst's collection of exotic animals – zebras, jaguars, lions, tigers, even an elephant for his guests to ride – swelled in size to become the world's largest private zoo. Hearst purchased the facade of a Roman temple and had it transported from Italy and reassembled on the site to form a stunning foreground to the Pacific. Here his guests sipped elegant drinks beside the 345,000-gallon Neptune Pool while surveying a spectacular view of the ocean. Many fortunate guests also enjoyed accommodation in one of three stucco guest houses—*Casa del Mar, Casa del Monte* and *Casa del Sol (Houses of the Sea, Mountain, Sun)*—ranging in size from a comfortable 2,500 to 5,350 square feet. The entire complex was neatly interconnected and linked to the outside world by one hundred telephones placed around the estate, even one discreetly concealed behind a tree. But the crown jewel of architect Morgan's castle complex was the centerpiece plaza and main residence *Casa Grande.* Massive at 68,500 square feet, this imitation of the Church of Santa Maria la Mayor in Ronda, Spain, actually fulfilled a very pragmatic function: Hearst needed a place to display the European art and furniture he had amassed in his travels. His collection overflowed his warehouses, and this grand structure would allow him to display his paintings, sculptures, and rare collectibles.

To this remote, fantastic castle, Hearst's train, cars, and plane brought a glittering array of guests such as Clark Gable, Greta Garbo, Cary Grant, Jimmy Stewart, Bob Hope, Franklin Roosevelt and Winston Churchill. There they admired the art and enjoyed the luxuries of the billiard room, the private movie theatre, and the beauty salon. Not every viewer proved admiring: Orson Welles's 1941 *Citizen Kane* was a thinly-veiled cinematic attack on Hearst and – through its presentation of Kane's ostentatious mansion Xanadu – on Hearst's beloved Castle. Aside from the occasional ungrateful guest, though, most visitors were amazed by the Enchanted Hill.

In August 1925, however, Welles's attack lay years in the future, and the San Simeon castle showed promise of fulfilling Hearst's every wish. So, what could possibly draw his interest to a dilapidated English castle when he was already assembling a castle over which he had entire design approval; at a beloved coastal location near the center of his California business operations; with a size and structure that would quite comfortably house his European art, furniture, and architectural collections?

The goad that drove him to contact Alice Head was from his reading of an innocuous magazine article that would have truly bored most readers: an article on the arcane history of armor. The apparently provocative magazine that fired his imagination was called *Country Life*. In the 1920s *Country Life* was *the* great arbiter of upper-class English taste, a quintessentially English magazine for the aristocratic reader. Often included as its frontispiece was what was casually known as the "Girls in Pearls" feature: the studio portrait of a debutante whose marriage had recently been announced. Within its pages, nobles could read about their fox hunts, their yachting competitions at Cowes, their parties, and their grouse-hunting in Scotland. A favorable profile of one's great country house or gardens was an acknowledged imprimatur fixing one's worthiness to be part of the elite social sphere. *Country Life* not only offered elegant gossip about the lives of the privileged but also handed down definitive cultural judgments as to tasteful house and garden design.

The April 2, 1921, issue of *Country Life* included an article about a remarkable collection of arms that was housed in St. Donat's, a castle in Wales. The writer of the article, F. H. (Francis Henry) Cripps-Day, had indeed waxed lyrical about armor and his article would naturally have some slight appeal to Hearst's ambition as a collector. He wrote approvingly about St. Donat's varied specimens of fashions in armor, its impressive collection of double-hander and claymore swords, and its "fine representative series" of maces. "This is not," Cripps-Day wrote fervently, "a collection limited to museum pieces and rare works of the craftsman's art, but rather a collection illustrating the whole history of European armour and arms, and a life-long study."

Still, the article would have remained a study of a somewhat fusty medieval topic had Cripps-Day not pointed out the one cultural treasure that Hearst did not possess and had not even understood before. It was a prize that would be beyond the reach of most men in the world and so became an irresistible quest for Hearst. At the conclusion of the article when Cripps-Day passionately rose to champion the cause of armorial collecting, he wrote the lines that caused Hearst to stop and reorder his passions: "the fascination of the study of armour is that it provides the *actual and personal setting* to the scene which the imagination is trying to reconstruct" [emphasis mine].

Hearst had been able to collect historical and artistic objects that were the envy of many great museums. But the context – " the actual and personal setting" at Hearst Castle – of these treasures, he had to concede, was new and derivative of many architectural styles: *La Cuesta Encantata* was undeniably a pastiche. As Hearst understood it, Cripps-Day was essentially arguing that *genuine objects in their original setting* have a powerful evocative authority that objects outside of their original context can only faintly echo. Hearst's American castle, no matter how wonderfully designed, would be inauthentic: it would be the faint echo rather than the powerful authority.

Cripps-Day ended his article with the pensive thought, "We wonder why there are so few collectors [of armor]." In ruminating over this article, Hearst apparently felt a metaphorical hurled gauntlet. He would not just be a collector of armor, furniture, paintings, and sculpture: he would acquire authenticity itself.

So, regardless of his stated indifference as to a specific castle and despite his businessman's instinct to look for the best bargain, Hearst trained his sights on that very castle in the west of Wales about which he had read: St. Donat's.

Like *La Cuesta Encantada*, St. Donat's sat on an elevation magisterially surveying water—in this case the Bristol Channel. Similarly, it was a collection of buildings and terraced elevations. But there the resemblance ended. This 12th century structure was undeniably medieval in structure and most amenities. Of heavy, rough gray stone, it had an inner court surrounded by a curtain wall and an outer wall punctuated by a tower and gate house, all topped with crenellations. A wide avenue swept up to its barbican entrance beside a dry moat. Solid, imposing, uncompromising, St. Donat's was far removed from the sunny, inviting Mediterranean look of *La Cuesta Encantada*. Clearly this was a place designed for warfare and domination. Where Hearst Castle at San Simeon had collected the styles of old Spain, Italy, and California, St. Donat's offered sheer, rugged authenticity.

Hearst bought it before the year had ended.

Once Hearst actually possessed this brooding medieval pile of stone that he had purchased sight unseen, he did not bother to visit it for years. He had it extensively renovated, bringing electricity not only to his estate but—like a grand country squire—sharing it with the surrounding area at a time when most homes lacked electricity. A hundred men worked on the Welsh project, digging a 150-foot pool that he did *not* want built in marble because it was not in "the character of the castle." Further, he instructed Head to acquire "parts of old, preferably Gothic buildings" instead of fabricating something new. And so, much of the décor added to the house was native to Britain, though the dismantling of Bradenstoke Priory for its wood eventually caused protest by the Society for the Protection of Ancient Buildings.

After three years of extensive restoration, Hearst finished refurbishing his authentic medieval castle. Finally laying eyes on it, he was charmed. He soon gave parties like the ones at *La Cuesta Encantada*, inviting celebrities such as Charlie Chaplin, Errol Flynn, Bob Hope, Douglas Fairbanks, and the young American John F. Kennedy. Exclusive London hotels such as Claridges and the Savoy supplied chefs and butlers. Here his paramour, silent screen star Marion Davies, presided over festivities without arousing U. S. press interest or the ire of his wife. Hearst felt the purchase to be a rousing success. The authentic medieval castle designed to repel foreign attacks and looting now welcomed genial guests to lavish food and comfortable lodging. George Bernard Shaw was to have said that St. Donat's was "what God would have built if he had had the money."

In St. Donat's, Hearst owned a genuine alternative to the eclectic California castle. He owned "the actual and personal setting to the scene which the imagination is trying to reconstruct": an authentic castle. Yet what did "authenticity" mean to wealthy men such as Hearst?

What this solid, historical castle expressed was power, confidence, and—implied in its authenticity—the cachet of the historic English upper class.

This American desire for authenticity, at heart, was an attempt to purchase a way into the English upper class by owning a great house. The desire was not unique to Americans, but Hearst's case perhaps best illustrates the attraction because his San Simeon castle clearly had all of the contents of many great houses. His persistence to move ahead and own St. Donat's as well helps us begin to describe the fascination with and cultural meaning of the English country houses and the aristocrats who lived in them. What St. Donat's and other British estates offered to Hearst and others of his economic class was an intangible asset that these successful businessmen and their families sought to acquire along with buildings, barns, lands, and artwork: a title in all but name.

Early nineteenth century American writers such as Emerson, Thoreau, and Whitman had claimed independence from the class traditions and distinction of the British. But American writers who followed them, such as Henry James and Edith Wharton, observed how imitation and envy of the British upper class was creeping back into the American upper class. America had its wealthy who, F. Scott Fitzgerald famously wrote, "are different from you and me." The working class who were the actual undergirding of any upper-class system clearly understood this difference. American wealth was placed on elaborate display in the necklace of fabulous "summer cottages" at Newport, at George Vanderbilt II's eponymous *Biltmore* in Asheville, and in other grand homes along the southern seacoast. There was even a parsing of the better wealth: Eastern versus Western, Northern versus Southern, Harvard-educated versus Princetonian. Edith Wharton's *Age of Innocence*, though a fictional piece, penetratingly recorded the strata of behavior, slights, and expectations that placed one happily at the heart of upper-class social life or beyond the pale.

So perhaps it became inevitable that the New Wealth of America began gazing fondly – or jealously – at the Old Wealth of Great Britain as Hearst, William Astor, and others came to do. Certainly, Americans could build great houses and create elaborate social structures; but America's democracy could never be as old or as titled as was Britain. This difference – politically repellent but socially irresistible to the New Wealth of America—became a point of fascination as the nineteenth century waned and the twentieth century exploded. The British upper-class system excluded or condescended to any who did not hold inherited wealth and title. Members within the system knew each other, married each other, and relied upon each other for social and political support. Great houses proved wealth and title. Strict social rules kept out interlopers.

But what happens if the wealth falters, if a great house no longer proves title and social class? What happens if the gilded cage of privilege is attacked or if the private affairs of the aristocrats become exposed to public judgment? At first glance such matters would seem like a tempest in a teacup. But if some of that spilled tea has the name Churchill or Mitford attached to it, the stakes change dramatically.

CHAPTER 2

THE HOUSE *IS*
THE FAMILY

On November 29, 1874, a very pregnant 22-year-old Jennie Jerome Churchill was dancing at the St. Andrews Ball at Blenheim Palace. Earlier in the day she had fallen ill at a shooting party, suffered a rough ride back to the Palace in a pony cart, and so no one expected to see her at the dance that evening. The beautiful woman, though, had had enough of the constraints and seclusions placed upon pregnant women. She had dutifully and discreetly kept secret her pregnancy at the time of her wedding to Randolph Churchill; she had spent her first seven months as Lady Churchill in increasing confinement. Now she was at one of the greatest country estates in England—an estate belonging to her father-in-law, the 7th Duke of Marlborough—and she was determined to enjoy herself.

Unfortunately, scarcely had the entertainment begun when unexpected labor pains commenced in earnest. Servants tried to help her return to her bedroom but could only make it as far as the first-floor ladies cloakroom. There was no chloroform to ease her pain, and so it was probably one of the most unnerving ends to any dance in history when guests had to sneak in while Lady Churchill lay "[sprawled on their] velvet capes and feather boas," and…deftly "draw [their wraps] from beneath her." After eight hours of labor, at 1:30 a.m., Jennie gave birth to a son, a boy who could possibly become master of this estate one day.

The London Times politely reported that the child was born prematurely.

The baby was, of course, Winston Leonard Spencer Churchill. As wartime Prime Minister of Britain, he would become the most admired political figure of the twentieth century, and so Blenheim Palace was undeniably an appropriately auspicious setting for his birth. However, it was only by chance that Winston was born at a great country estate—and it was only by chance that his ancestral home was grand at all. This ducal seat, a masterpiece in the English Baroque style, and an architectural behemoth covered by seven acres of roof was a *gift* that got greatly out of hand.

Winston's ancestor was the 1st Duke of Marlborough, the dashing John Churchill. Though born of a prominent family and proven as a distinguished general, John had a spotty record of political success. He once backed the Catholic King James and then completely reversed his allegiance to support the Protestant King William and Queen Mary. In fact, John Churchill spent time in the Tower of London precisely because he never could quite prove his political fidelity to the satisfaction of the King. Though brilliantly putting down the Monmouth Rebellion and distinguishing himself in the Nine Years' war, this general could not translate military strategy into political savvy.

Even his courtship of Sarah Jennings showed how easily John could be outmaneuvered in a game of wits. He had intended to take Sarah as a lover; however, the 17-year-old outwitted him with the result that in 1677 they were married. As the recent movie *The Favourite* demonstrated, Sarah was the making of John Churchill. As the wife of a prominent lord, she employed that same pre-marital shrewdness on behalf of her husband in helping protect him from the continued whiff of royal distrust that darkened his career at the court of William and Mary. Instinctively – and some would say brutally – Sarah navigated the intrigues of court to keep her husband both informed and at the forefront of royal attention. The poet Alexander Pope wrote of her: "Offend her, and she knows not to forgive." Ultimately, her most astute political move was to link her fortunes to those of Princess Anne.

Anne, whose sister was the Queen, endlessly had to battle her sister and brother-in-law to be granted any money or personal independence. Sarah Churchill put her considerable negotiating skills to use in gaining concessions for her royal friend. When Anne finally ascended as Queen, partly in gratitude for Sarah's loyalty, she soon found reasons to raise John Churchill to the highest and most exclusive order of the peerage, the rank of Duke of Marlborough. In 1705 the Marlboroughs further endeared themselves to Queen Anne when

John defeated the French and Bavarians at the Battle of Blenheim in Bavaria. This victory ended France's attempt to unite with Spain and so set Britain on the path to becoming the premier European power.

To find some adequate expression of gratitude for John's victory at Blenheim, Queen Anne turned to her friend Sarah to see what might be pleasing to the Churchills. Here Sarah boldly called in all of her social capital: she persuaded Anne to bestow upon John the gift of a country house and 2,700 acres in Oxfordshire. The resulting gift took nearly three decades to build, employed over 1,500 workmen, and became – because of its breathtaking scale—the only non-royal country house in England to hold the title of *palace*. To the eventual horror of Anne and the British government, it also ballooned to over five times the initial estimated cost and ultimately estranged the Marlboroughs from Queen Anne. In 1711 they went into exile, only returning to the country the day after Anne's death in 1714.

But the gift had been given. A later royal ruler, King George III, would look down from a hilltop towards the palace and remark with a mixture of awe and royal chagrin, "We have nothing to equal this."

Blenheim Palace became an emphatic statement of Churchillian power and wealth. No one could doubt that this English general had thrashed the French. Entering the palace area from the extensive grounds, one passed beneath a massive Arch of Triumph modeled after the Roman Arch of Titus. Atop the entrance pediment to the palace stood a statue of Britannia with two chained French captives cringing beneath her. A lower roof displayed an English lion devouring the French rooster. If that were not enough, John Churchill had placed at the south portico a 30-ton marble bust of Louis XIV that he had looted from the French—and he always, always made a point of sitting with his back to it. Each feature of the palace was expensive, massive, and calculated to awe.

The vestiges of a warrior architecture now signaled not an unassailable barbican but an unassailable class structure. Where St. Donat's Castle in Wales had been constructed with towers for spotting enemies and crenellations to protect its archers, Blenheim's newer Palace had more social goals in mind: *its* tower housed a clock and *its* battlements were elegantly decorative. The 320 rooms in the interior of the palace emphasized the Churchills' formidable economic status. Blenheim's entrance hall soared to over four stories in height. The library, stocked with rare first editions, exceeded half the length of a football field. Walls were crowded with great works of art ranging from Raphael's *Ansidei Madonna* to Van Dyck's equestrian painting of Charles I.

Not satisfied with simply creating an imposing structure, each succeeding duke reshaped the landscape to his taste as well. A dry-stone wall running for nearly nine miles around the ancient forests and lush fields of the estate represented a formidable land barrier. In the 1760s the 4th Duke employed the landscape darling of the aristocrats, Lancelot "Capability" Brown, to reshape the grounds into an even more aesthetic framework for the great house. Unfettered, Brown dammed a river, formed a lake, constructed a series of cascades, and diverted a stream to flow under what some people considered to be the most beautiful stone bridge in Britain. The bridge had actually been a thirty-room estate house; but Brown flooded and submerged the lower stories, surfaced the roof, and made it a carriageway. Eventually, on a height in the park rose a 134-foot-high Column of Victory honoring the 1st Duke, an exclamation point to the Churchills' imperial greatness. Generations of Marlboroughs claimed nature, architecture, wealth, and art as their sovereign birthright, as offerings framing the family's glory.

Blenheim, impressive and awe-inspiring though it was, was only one of thousands of stately houses constructed with the aim of inserting a family into that elite aristocratic social class walled about by wealth, title, family ties, and temperament. Because these families thirsted to proclaim their prominence and to meld into the aristocracy, they embraced the common architectural and landscape vocabulary of that class, often sharing the same designers. John Vanbrugh, the architect of Blenheim, had two decades earlier designed Castle Howard in Yorkshire. The Howard family reflected the elegance of the Baroque style and evoked a scale similar to Blenheim's. The private mausoleum at Castle Howard equaled the cost and size of any of Christopher Wren's London churches; its immense entry courtyard wrapped by facing wings of the house would be recreated in the expansive plaza in front of Blenheim; and like Blenheim, Castle Howard reflected the elegance of the Baroque style. There in Yorkshire the planners also wrestled with the natural landscape to subdue it to the Howard family's will. The central grounds of the house ended in a ha-ha, a sunken fence designed to separate the private part of the estate while preserving an uninterrupted view. Not satisfied with that unimpeded view afforded by the ha-ha, Vanbrugh razed estate villages, a church, and a ruined castle in order to create the best view—the perfect, aesthetic view he considered desirable for his employers. The importance of this single stately house became so immense that by 1845 the estate even had its own railway station.

Other designers consciously linked their house designs or landscapes to prominent structures or to preeminent families. The Carnarvon family hired "Capability" Brown to design a park with expansive views calculated to show the Carnarvons' natural dominance over all that they surveyed. Then, in an overt effort to link the Carnarvons to the highest ranks of government, the 3rd Earl hired Sir Charles Barry, architect of the Palace of Westminster, who remodeled Highclere castle in the style of the Houses of Parliament.

Capability Brown was also hired to landscape the great house Longleat in Wiltshire for the 1st Marquess of Bath where – among other additions – he planted 91,00 trees in a single year. When he was hired to landscape the Buckinghamshire estate of Stowe House, Brown created a Grecian Valley for the 1st Marquess of Buckingham by having workmen use wheelbarrows to haul away nearly 24 tons of soil and rock. At Heveningham in Suffolk, for the 2nd Baronet Sir Gerard Vanneck, Capability Brown—like Vanbrugh at Castle Howard—relocated villages, moved fully-grown trees, and raised the height of a vast lawn by twelve feet, all with the support of manual labor. Other landscape designers enthusiastically followed Brown's lead: landscape designer Henry Ernest Milner even installed a sandstone model of the Matterhorn at Friar Park.

In sum, stately houses, their lands, and their designers were hallmarks of a class that consciously set itself apart as an exclusive and superior class. Their peers—and jealous outsiders—understood that these great country houses were verifiable evidence, not just of wealth, but of a greatness that had evolved through a complex, prestigious history.

Just the fact of owning large masses of land made a tremendous difference in concentrating wealth, exercising power, and identifying the elite — and a very small number of men owned a tremendous amount of land. In the 1880s — just prior to Winston Churchill's birth — sixty peers each owned 50,000 acres of land; fourteen of them owned in excess of 100,000 acres each. Even a relatively minor peer, George Herbert, the 5th Earl of Carnarvon, was not atypical in owning houses or estates in London, Hampshire, Somerset, Nottinghamshire, and Highclere Castle in Derbyshire. Loftier nobles owned vaster lands. The estate of William Cavendish, the 7th Duke of Devonshire, extended to nearly 200,000 acres. But the 2nd Duke of Sutherland trumped all other peers: he owned a stunning 1.3 million acres. The location of some land — in cities, different counties, even in Scotland, Wales, or Ireland — proved more valuable in the course of time as well. Not surprisingly, in 1880 land mainly in London owned by the 1st Duke of Westminster was valued at £290,000 (approximately $33 million). In 2019 its worth to his descendant, the 7th Duke of Westminster, was $13 billion.

The upper class profited not just from agriculture but also from cottage and shop rents, mineral drilling and excavation, and exports to countries acquired in the expansion of the British Empire. Their vast estates and labor force could take full advantage of the agricultural advancements made in the 18th century such as Jethro Tull's seed-planter, Charles Townshed's guide to crop rotation, the Hargreaves-Higg's spinning jenny that operated multiple spindles at a time. Initially the landed gentry even benefited from industrial advances such as James Watts' steam engine that could bore mine shafts for coal mining on their property. The advent of farm machinery meant that fewer laborers were needed on the farms, a change which flooded the factories, mines, and great houses with cheap labor. Service jobs in the great country houses seemed safer than mines and preferable to risking the poverty and dislocation of city life; and so, for decades, the great houses also had an affordable work force.

Land provided the foundation for much British law and government. As Barbara Tuchman has observed, "They [The English lords] had learned the practice of government from the possession of great estates, and they undertook to manage the affairs of the nation as inevitably and unquestionably as beavers build a dam. It was their ordained role and natural task." These lords who had learned governance from their personal estate management insured that government policies protected and favored those country estates. Landed gentry constituted one half of the Parliament, and the (hereditary) House of Lords had full legislative veto power over laws. At their zenith in Prime Minister Arthur Balfour's Cabinet in 1902, the British landed establishment constituted 15 of the 20-member cabinet. Because peers dominated the Parliament, the laws protected their land both at home and in the far-flung reaches of the Empire.

CHAPTER 3

OF EAGLES
AND GULLS

A great house, though a tremendous achievement in itself, was only part of the aristocratic equation. Gaining a title and vast properties proved more challenging because that was generally the work of one's ancestors. In early times, rulers used physical strength to cudgel followers into submission. By the Middle Ages, when muscle alone was sometimes less effective, kings were forced to cudgel their royal minds for additional ways to keep followers loyal to them in war and in peace. One remedy that cost a king nothing was to bestow generous gifts of newly-conquered lands. A significant instance of this scheme occurred in 1066 at the last successful conquest of England. William the Conqueror distributed seized lands to bind his knights to himself through their gratitude, self-interest in maintaining their spoils, and a shrewd hope for future rewards. Over time this vassal system evolved into a more complicated scheme with more tempting rewards in the form of increasingly important ranks. In this manner kings forged an enduring link between the ownership of *land* and a system of *titles* that was hierarchical, prestigious, and – perhaps most important – hereditary.

In fact, family title became the hallmark of the English upper class. Anyone born into this class was reared to know the ranks and to gauge how much respect – or, alternatively, how much condescension – to accord to other members in the class. Some modest designations such as knighthoods existed, but they were usually bestowed for the lifetime of the honoree: hereditary ranks were far more exclusive. The lowest inherited rank was that of Baron and Baroness, whose family could claim to write the word "Honorable" in front of their names when corresponding or being announced at a ball. The next higher rank was that of viscount and viscountess. Superior to that rank was an earl and his wife, the countess. A marquess and marchioness ranked above an earl, and their properties were called marquessates. But the pinnacle of this system was the rank of duke and duchess, whose prestige and wealth eclipsed all those beneath them.

By the 1800s membership in this exclusive, titled social class—the peerage—had become so complicated that publications such as Debrett's *Peerage and Baronetage* and Burke's *Peerage* were established as final authorities for stating the genealogy, courtesies, and signs of respect for the various ranks.

Despite the aristocrats' cutting enforcement of social protocols and lineage rankings, some great families could sometimes push the boundaries of acceptance. Jennie Jerome Churchill attended the legendary Devonshire Ball in 1897 dressed as Empress Theodora, in a gown designed by the couturier Jean Worth of Paris. Emeralds and diamonds dangled from her headdress. However, from some perspectives, she should not have been invited. She was an American and not born into the English upper class. But Jennie was what would later be called a *buccaneer*, and her ticket for admission to the ball was her late husband, Randolph Churchill.

The social meaning of the word *buccaneer* arose from an unfinished 1938 novel by Edith Wharton's titled *The Buccaneers* (1938). Though her work was fiction, Wharton accurately recorded a quandary that faced the English upper class near the end of the nineteenth century: the American social assault on the English elite. Gilded Age capitalists such as Cornelius Vanderbilt, John D. Rockefeller, and Andrew Mellon had amassed great fortunes and built great houses in America that could compare with those in England; but the English owned authentic castles and had an attribute that tantalized because it was so impossible for Americans: a title. The attraction of an English title took on the lure of the Holy Grail to these American entrepreneurs. Wharton accurately described in fiction what had happened in fact: young American heiresses under the supervision of ambitious mothers streamed to England in an attempt to leap that hurdle into the elite circles of British society. The buccaneers, for their part, were genuine temptations to English lords because an impoverished noble had the chance to replenish his coffers, repair his estate, and maintain his accustomed lifestyle if he would make the socially-demeaning concession of marrying outside of his social circle.

American heiress Consuelo Vanderbilt told the story – which may be apocryphal – that in 1938 her family locked her in a room until she agreed to marry Charles "Sunny" Spencer-Churchill, the 9th Duke of Marlborough (Winston Churchill's cousin). There was no doubt that William Vanderbilt paid the Duke a dowry of $67 million in stock shares with guaranteed minimum dividends, and an annual allowance of $100,000 (2019 value). Consuelo could justifiably feel ill-treated. Her dowry restored a crumbling Blenheim Palace but did little to gain her husband's affections: he never even considered breaking his liaison with his lover Gladys Deacon. Consuelo Vanderbilt's case was dramatic, but nearly ten per cent of marriages among the titled during this time period were to American heiresses.

There also was "constant pressure not to do "'The Wrong Thing." This second revealing story was told about Consuelo Vanderbilt, new Duchess of Marlborough: "Once, at a party at Blenheim Palace, her husband's seat, Consuelo was unsure of the sequence in which the Ladies should be withdrawing from the dining room. Not wanting to appear rude, she dithered in the doorway, only to be shoved in the back by a furious marchioness, who hissed at her, 'It is quite as vulgar to hang back as to jump ahead.'" The new Duchess had run into a social buzzsaw that was honed to a razor's edge: the sharp observance of the distinctions within the aristocratic social system. Ignorance of the proper courtesies invariably resulted in embarrassment. Transgressing the distinctions too much meant exclusion and social annihilation.

Sunny Spencer-Churchill was an apex aristocrat with a huge estate, rents from tenants, masses of valuable art, and an hereditary title. English upper-class families such as the Churchills retained their lands and wealth to a far greater degree and for centuries longer than did their peers on the continent of Europe. Three factors made that possible. First, Britain never experienced such cultural cataclysms as the French Revolution or the Russian Revolution that stripped inherited land and wealth from aristocrats. Second, the English upper class benefited extraordinarily from the empire-building of their country. However, one crucial cultural concept solidified the English system of wealth in a way that few Europeans ever achieved: the principle of inheritance called *primogeniture,* where the eldest son was primary in every respect. In Europe the eldest son would inherit the family title, but family lands were often divided among many male heirs. That division did not occur in the English upper-class system. In England, the eldest son inherited the title, houses, lands, and all other properties while his siblings might receive an allowance from him. Primogeniture allowed the titled English families to maintain their amassed wealth, especially vast tracts of land. In the case of Winston Churchill, though his grandfather was the 7th Duke of Marlborough, Winston was unlikely to inherit Blenheim because the title and lands went to the elder brother (Winston's uncle George) and his sons. Winston would only have gained the title of Duke if his uncle's children were all female. Primogeniture allowed the great estates to remain intact and concentrated the wealth in one titled family line. As any observer could see, the vast lands were physical representations of a superior economic class that—when combined with the scale and magnificence of their great houses—established an insuperable class barrier.

In London, aristocrats at their exclusive clubs on Pall Mall — the Carlton, Athenaeum, Turf, White's, or Boodles — could chat privately about laws and strike agreements among themselves. Additionally, because titled families married within their social circle, peers could count upon their relatives for financial, political, and social assistance. For example, in 1895 the Secretary of War, Lord Lansdowne, was a relative of both the Secretary for India and the Lord President of the Council. Even in Winston Churchill's time, his son-in-law Duncan Sandys was his Minister of Housing and Local Government; and his successor as Prime Minister, Anthony Eden, was his niece Clarissa's husband.

The Dukes of Marlborough lived in the airy heights of the system. Their cousins, the Mitfords – with the family rank of Baron – flew in the same skies as the Churchills, but their rank and wealth were modest in the scales. If Churchills were eagles, the Mitfords were gulls.

The Mitford ancestors had held land in Northumberland even prior to William the Conqueror's invasion, but those lands had been diminished through regional wars. The prominence of the family was regained in the nineteenth century through the accomplishments of Algernon Bertram "Bertie" Freeman-Mitford, cousin to the poet Algernon Swinburne. Mitford was part of the bureaucratic underpinning necessary to Empire-building. In the 1860s he served in the diplomatic corps in St. Petersburg, Shanghai, and—most importantly—in Japan. When Bertie returned to England, he was credited with developing a vogue for Japanese culture through his popularization of the tragedy of "The Forty-Seven Ronin" and his advice to Gilbert and Sullivan on their popular opera *The Mikado*. His official work continued when he became secretary to HM Office of Works at the time of the restoration of the Tower of London and the landscaping of Hyde Park.

In 1874, Mitford married Lady Clementine Olgivy, daughter of the 10th Earl of Airlie. Although married, like many aristocrats, Bertie did not feel constrained by conventional morality. He was said to have fathered children by a geisha while in Japan and to have had an affair with Clementine's sister, Blanche. In fact, Mitford is listed as one of the possible fathers of Blanche's daughter, also named Clementine. In that case he would not only have been the uncle but also the father of the woman who later married Winston Churchill.

By 1886 Bertie had had the good fortune to inherit valuable lands upon the death of a distant cousin. Almost immediately, he translated his new wealth into funds for rehabilitating a Gloucestershire country house, Batsford House, in the neo-Tudor style. Further establishing himself as a country squire, Bertie took up horse breeding, farming, and yachting. However, the year 1902 heralded his crowning achievement as a patriarch. His contributions to the Empire while within the diplomatic corps were rewarded with the honor that would forever secure his family's place in aristocratic society. Albeit a gull among eagles, Algernon Bertram Freeman-Mitford was granted the title of 1st Baron Redesdale.

The Baron and Baroness Redesdale had nine children, five of whom were boys. Because of primogeniture, Bertie naturally gave much attention to Clement, his eldest son, and some to second son David. Clement went to the prestigious, expensive Eton; the Baron's younger son David attended the second-tier school Radley. Clement was intelligent, poised, and all his father could have wished for in an heir. David, though handsome and passionate about country sports, loathed his school, developed a fiery temper, failed entrance exams to Sandhurst, and at age seventeen was sent to Ceylon (Sri Lanka) in hopes that he could find success in the tea business. After four years, David seemed a failure even at that. In 1898, though, the Boer War beckoned both Clement and David. Clement served with distinction with the 10th Hussars, and David served in the Northumberland Fusiliers under Lord Brabazon, a former commanding officer of young Winston Churchill. David survived a leg wound in 1900, but in 1901 he was wounded so severely that he lost a lung and was subsequently invalided home.

Upon his return David rekindled a friendship with young Sydney Bowles, a spunky young woman who, since her mother's death when Sydney was eight, had managed her father's household. By no measure could one say that her upbringing was conventional. After his wife's death, Thomas Bowles took his children to sea for the next six years, stopping at Middle Eastern and European ports of call. When they finally settled in London, Bowles involved his children with his campaigns to become a Member of Parliament. He gave them instruction in the running of *Vanity Fair, The Lady*, and other magazines in his publishing empire. Sydney, though sobered by home responsibilities, grew up to be sociable and a beauty; painter Paul-Cesar Helleu painted several portraits of her. She was introduced into society as a debutante and had a lively social circle. Several of her beaux and friends were killed during the Boer War, so perhaps it was not surprising that she was drawn to the man on whom she had once had a teenage crush. She and David traveled in the same social circles, shared a sense of humor, and were generally regarded as a handsome couple.

David and Sydney married on February 6, 1904. As a second son with no real job skills, David felt compelled to accept his father-in-law's offer of a job at *The Lady*. He loathed the office work and longed for enough money to escape. Instead, on November 28 of that year, he was greeted with the birth of the first of their seven children. He had no prospect of being anything other than an office worker, a dismal low within his social class.

Clement was the golden boy and David the dismal failure. Their fortunes would radically change.

CHAPTER 4

"I HAVE THE CROWN
OF ENGLAND IN MY POCKET"

While David Mitford longed for hunting and pleasant rustication, Winston Churchill's family history was a revealing and personal demonstration of how the extravagance of this aristocracy operated. Winston was born in a time of "imperial heroes," men "whose feats were held up to the nation as examples of how men of courage and determination could shape the destiny of that noblest achievement of mankind, the Empire." Winston saw himself in the mold of such men and regarded his father Randolph as such a man as well. In his quest for greatness, Randolph Churchill exploited the advantages of his social class and courted disaster by ignoring some of its most jealously-protected strictures. Years later, his son would follow suit.

Randolph Henry Spencer-Churchill was the third son of the 7th Duke of Marlborough, and so primogeniture determined that his title would be the modest Right Honorable Lord Randolph Churchill and that he would always be the (relatively) poor relation of his eldest brother. He attended Eton – that exclusive school upon whose fields were to be found future prime ministers – and though he was a witty, impetuous companion, he was indifferent about his studies. When he later managed to enter Merton College, Oxford, he devoted himself much more to the aristocratic fun of horses and foxhunting than to his studies. Randolph bridged any deficit with his charm, satiric wit, and impeccable dress. His face reflected a man who quickly knew his opinions: his large eyes stared; his nostrils flared slightly; his lower lip protruded confidently under an immaculately waxed walrus mustache. He was so confident of his status that he would wear polka-dot bow ties for formal portraits. That self-assurance often ran into recklessness. He made great friends at Merton and readily set the standard for drunkenness at champagne dinners. He tweaked school authorities by smoking in forbidden areas. He and friends were caught breaking windows at the local hotel. His wit and an extraordinary energy made him a natural leader among his peers.

Fortunately, Randolph loved to read and memorize great speeches—an example his son Winston would follow—and so his academic career slowly began to progress. He eventually improved his academic achievement and graduated with solid marks though with an indifferent reputation among his professors. Then, like other wealthy young men, he followed his graduation with the Grand Tour: a year-and-a-half of travel through France, Italy, and Austria. Life unfolded for Randolph with ease and liquid pleasure until his father the Duke finally said that he must settle to a profession. In quick order, Randolph ran and won election to Parliament from his father's district, married a wealthy and beautiful American, and welcomed the birth of his first son, Winston.

Randolph had met Jennie Jerome at the Cowes yachting days during the 1873 Season. She was gorgeous, witty, and much sought-after by all of the young men competing in the yacht races around the Isle of Wight. She was a prize far superior to any racing cup, and Randolph pursued her with all of his charm. Within three days of meeting, they were engaged – and Randolph's family was apoplectic. First, Randolph had not taken the step of asking his father's permission. Second, Jennie was from an American family unfamiliar to the Churchills and their social group. The Duke wrote to Randolph, "Never was there such an illustration of the adage *love is blind*,' for you seem blind to all consequences in order that you may pursue your passion; blind to the relative consequences as regards your family; and blind to the trouble you are heaping on Mamma and me by the anxieties this act [of engagement] has produced… ."

Jenny's father, Leonard Jerome, was acceptably wealthy for the Marlborough's social set (he offered a $4 million dowery); but he was, in the view of the 7th Duke of Marlborough, a "vulgar kind of man" involved in the stock market. Jerome was, honestly, a rogue. He had made and lost millions of dollars through speculation and questionable business practices. He had several lovers. He was undeniably American. The investigations of the Duke's men confirmed that great weight was "against a connection."

Transatlantic fireworks crackled. Leonard, hearing of the Duke's opposition, cabled Mrs. Jerome, "CONSENT WITHDRAWN." The lovers desperately tried to soothe their respective families and endured separation when the Duke sent Randolph to Ireland. Ironically, it was the Parliamentary race of 1874 that seemed to save the engagement. Randolph won the Marlborough's traditional seat of Woodstock, so the Duke felt reassured that his son might be mature and agreed that a Member of Parliament should have a wife. He proposed to pay all of Randolph's debts and his expenses as a Member of Parliament. Mr. Jerome, for his part, settled an annual allowance of $180,000 on his *daughter* – a proposal angrily opposed by the Churchill lawyers as un-English (for being settled on the bride, not the groom) – and, therefore, unthinkable. Negotiations were at loggerheads. However, the passionate couple cut short all financial negotiations by marrying in Paris on April 14, 1874. Jennie was probably pregnant at the time. Although the *London Times* officially noted the birth as premature, even Winston would later joke, "Although present on the occasion [of my birth], I have no clear recollection of the events leading up to it."

Randolph, though delighted to have an heir, like most men of his time pursued his career and interests largely without contact with his sons Winston and, later, John. Instead, he translated his high spirits from college days into fiery rhetoric in the halls of Parliament. His striking speeches quickly broadened his political influence, but his impetuosity promised to end his career almost before it began. In 1875 Randolph's older brother George was attempting to extricate himself from a love affair with Lady Aylesford. Lord Aylesford had discovered the affair and angrily threatened to divorce his wife and implicate George. In the meantime, Randolph claimed to have possession of love letters to Lady Aylesford from an even more prominent lover, the Prince of Wales. Randolph crowed, "I have the Crown of England in my pocket." He took the letters to the Prince's wife, Alexandra, in hopes she would apply pressure on Lord Aylesford before public exposure of George's affair. Instead he was soon confronted by a royal emissary, Lord Hartington (who, ironically, was engaged in an affair with the Duchess of Manchester). Hartington burned the letters in Randolph's presence and informed him that the Prince and Princess of Wales were angry beyond measure. Randolph and Jenny made a strategic retreat by taking an extended tour of Canada and the United States. Prime

Minister Disraeli then sent Randolph away to Ireland as an unofficial secretary to Randolph's father, the Duke. The affair itself ended with Lord Aylesford divorcing his wife; George ignored Lady Aylesford, and she died penniless. Randolph discreetly and dutifully kept to his work in Ireland.

Aside from providing a cooling-off period away from the Prince of Wales, Randolph's years in Ireland provided him with a practical political education. He saw first-hand the issues involved in the conflict over Irish self-rule and developed the view that some self-rule at the local level might be feasible. When Randolph finally returned to Parliament, he had a more mature view on another issue as well, arguing that Conservatives should take stock of changing demographics and attempt to attract working men's votes. He gained the reputation of being an energetic, brilliant politician with the one liability of an overly-hot temper. He distinguished himself in Parliament to the point that by 1885 he was appointed Secretary of State for India. There the aggressive young Secretary soon pushed for an invasion of what remained of Burma to add it to the Indian Raj. He was an empire-builder, and his son would follow him in attempting to maintain that Empire.

Finally, at age thirty-seven, Randolph was appointed to the high office of Chancellor of the Exchequer, a position that placed him at one remove from the chance of becoming prime minister. This time his temper and self-confidence fatally destroyed his career. He was curt, even rude, in questioning Prime Minister Salisbury's judgement. At the same time, he paid little attention to the details of the government's budget over which he had supervision: "I could never make out what those damned dots [decimals] meant." Instead, he turned to making policy for himself and sent budgets to Salisbury that the Prime Minister firmly rejected. Randolph then issued an ultimatum requiring an acceptance of his budget without change. To draw a line under the matter, he wrote his resignation and handed it to Salisbury, confident that the Prime Minister would collapse his objections rather than accept the resignation.

To Randolph's utter shock, the Prime Minister accepted the resignation.

This resignation meant political ruin for Randolph. His political career and his health seemed to drain away. He traveled to South Africa for his health and sent his travel journals home for publication. Nothing seemed to help. He died at age forty-five on January 24, 1894. Historians still debate whether the cause of death was syphilis contracted during his Oxford days or a brain tumor, but his son Winston always viewed the political death as primary cause of the physical one.

By Randolph's untimely death, twenty-year-old Winston had had scarcely a half-dozen full conversations with his father. One of the lengthiest talks had been about Winston's passion for re-enacting the Battles of Blenheim and Waterloo with his 1,500 toy soldiers. Randolph decided that the army might hold Winston's future and sent him toward it; Winston would always relish war, savor any good fight. But Randolph died before Winston could prove himself to his father. From one perspective, Winston's entire life reflected his idolizing of his father, his taking up of his father's political views, and his working to rehabilitate his father's reputation. Winston would even name his son Randolph.

Randolph Churchill left Jenny, Winston, and John a debt-encumbered estate of £10.5 million (2019 value). By upper class standards, with such a relatively modest income Winston would have to navigate the social waters quite carefully to achieve any prominence at all.

Fortunately for Winston, Jennie Jerome Churchill's beauty and social connections so dazzled the titled, awe-inspiring English gods that Winston was to lack for nothing.

CHAPTER 5

THE SEASON

Dozens of elegant carriages rolled one after the other into Piccadilly on a warm July 2nd night. Their gleaming doors opened and seven hundred glittering party-goers descended onto the steps of one of the most prestigious addresses in London. By the time they were folded back into those carriages in the wee hours of the morning, they had attended a ball so magnificent in scale and concept that it highlighted the 1897 social season and was etched in English aristocratic memory. Nearly a century later the 11th Duchess of Devonshire, Deborah Mitford, would give a ball evoking the glory of this occasion.

The location of the 1897 party was Devonshire House, the fabulous London town home of the 8th Duke and Duchess of Devonshire; and the occasion was Queen Victoria's Diamond Jubilee. It was a good thing that the Queen did not attend.

When her husband Prince Albert died in 1861, Victoria had taken to widow's weeds and turned her grief into worship of her husband, even to the point of having his valet clean and set out Albert's clothes each day. She withdrew from public life, emerging only to burden her family and subjects with a depressing sense of duty and earnestness. The Devonshires' enthusiastic plans, ostensibly to honor her fifty-year reign, really took no notice of the Queen's dour tastes. Despite Victoria's decades-long model of soberness, a sense of play had permeated the upper class through such avenues as the wit of Jane Austen, the irony of Oscar Wilde, the cheery silliness of the popular Gilbert and Sullivan musicals, and the possibilities created by wealth. The Devonshires wanted a costume ball.

The design of Devonshire House reflected the difference between the nobles' public image of Victorian sobriety and their private, extravagant social life. The house was a plain, brick, rectangular building in the balanced Palladian style and lacking in much ornamentation. The interior, by contrast, had a layout designed with an eye towards entertaining. Guests who entered the ground floor entrance then ascended the stunning "Crystal Staircase" of glass handrails and newel posts. After greeting their host and hostess, they entered a gilded ballroom, circulated into the 40-foot-long library, or admired the Duke's collection of engraved gems in his sitting room. The Devonshire invitation had encouraged guests to appear in "allegorical or historical costume before 1815." Attendees understood the challenge of the invitation and did not disappoint.

The Duke himself appeared as Emperor Charles V, and the Duchess made a jaw-dropping entrance as Queen Zenobia of Palmyra carried in a sedan chair by costumed servants. Some costumes were so elaborate as to be almost unsupportable. The Countess of Westmoreland, dressed as Hebe, wore a stuffed eagle on her shoulder. Fanny Ronalds, representing Euterpe, the muse of music, wore a lighted lyre on her head. Figures ranged from Horace Walpole, King Arthur, Catherine the Great of Russia, and Scheherazade, to the Doge of Venice. The Prince of Wales was grand and handsome as the Grand Master of the Knights of Malta; his brother, the Duke of York, impressed as Clifford, Earl of Cumberland. Lady Wolverton came as Britannia and several Cleopatras appeared.

No one had caviled at accepting the invitation to this ball even though most invitees probably knew the gossip that Louisa, this current Duchess of Devonshire, had been this Duke's lover for thirty years while she was still married to the Duke of Manchester. When Manchester finally died, she had married Devonshire and had become, people quipped, the "Double Duchess." Many indiscretions could be overlooked *if* the lovers were members of the upper class and *if* they were discreet.

Parties such as the Devonshire Ball were proving grounds separating the true patricians from social climbers. In fact, the annual series of social tests came to be known as The Season. To use a metaphor, The Season was the social racecourse where thoroughbreds would be recognized for their lineage and judged for their performance. Its original schedule was guided by the annual movements of the Royal Family and the schedule of Parliament. Later, Parliament tailored its sessions to accommodate The Season. "'Everywhere one met friends and kinsfolk,' wrote Winston [Churchill]. 'The leading figures of Society were in many cases the leading statesmen in Parliament, and also the leading sportsmen on the Turf. [Prime Minister] Lord Salisbury was accustomed scrupulously to avoid calling a Cabinet when there was racing at Newmarket, and the House of Commons made a practice of adjourning for the Derby.'"

The Season had its beginnings with the first grand presentation of a group of young ladies to a monarch – in this case, to Queen Charlotte on the occasion of her birthday in 1780. Over time this practice became viewed as the official debut of a young lady, usually at age eighteen. By the nineteenth century The Season officially began in May with the royal presentation and a series of balls during which debutantes could meet eligible bachelors of their class. The cost of a debut could be witheringly expensive because the requisite long-term preparation included study at exclusive schools such as Roedean, Cheltenham, and Sherborne; a "finishing" year abroad in France, Germany, or Switzerland for exposure to art, languages, and social protocols; and finally, the expense of a ball for two to three hundred people. A wardrobe for The Season, if designed by Worth of Paris, could cost as much as half a million in today's dollars. Debutantes needed every possible advantage, because in this society, everything from wardrobe to curtsys was imbued with social coding. If a lady wore "a crescent instead of a tiara [it] would infallibly have brought down a rebuke from the Prince of Wales… ." Every social act held meaning.

The first hurdle for debutantes was the presentation at court, and training for this particular event was both nerve-wracking and thorough. The best place to learn how to curtsy was considered to be at the *barre* in the Vacani School of Dancing in Knightsbridge, where one practiced how to put "the left foot behind the right, leaning the weight on to the right foot, bending the knees, sinking down and rising up in one fluid movement." Dress for the evening was strictly prescribed: each young lady entered the presence of the royals wearing "a short-sleeved white evening dress with a train…between 2 and 3 ½ yards long held in place by a headdress of three white ostrich plumes carefully arranged in the style of the Prince of Wales feathers." On the evening of the ceremony, elegant carriages or cars bearing the debutantes and their sponsors trailed down Pall Mall towards Buckingham Palace with throngs of onlookers jostling to see the dresses and identify faces. At precisely nine-thirty, the ceremony began. Each debutante and her sponsor were announced by full, formal title; each would execute a flawless curtsy; and – if they were favored – the Prince, King, or Queen might give a brief compliment or acknowledge their family ties. This moment placed the royal imprimatur upon these young women, who were now deemed acceptable for society and for a privileged marriage.

In the succeeding weeks, parents of the debutantes gave balls in London to showcase their daughters and their qualities. Families such as the Devonshires could use their town home; others rented large houses; eventually, it became acceptable to rent the ballrooms of exclusive hotels such as Claridges or the Dorchester. The glittering town homes whose addresses included Mayfair and Park Lane were reminders of the social line that parvenus still found difficult to cross. Country estates offered even more extravagant possibilities. In 1939 the Duke and Duchess of Marlborough gave a ball at Blenheim Palace for their daughter Lady Sarah Spencer-Churchill and invited 1,000 guests to dance and enjoy food and fountains of champagne.

By the twentieth century a definite pattern had coalesced: "Night after night, the streets of Mayfair and nearby Belgravia were clogged with cars tended by liveried drivers" delivering young men in white tie, tails, and white gloves to the balls that began at ten o'clock. At the balls "each girl carried a dance program with a pencil attached by a ribbon. The programs were numbered 1 to 20, and the boys scribbled their names next to the numbers, signifying which dance they would like to serve as partner." Some of the more daring debutantes, such as the Churchill cousins, the Mitfords, would slip out to a club and return "before the orchestra played 'God Save the King' and everyone stood at attention before going home."

There was no question but that this debut time was intended to grade the quality of debutantes. One former debutante, Angela Lambert, remarked that "'The Season . . .gave a girl a chance to prove herself and make her mark in a few short months, knowing that whatever impression she created might remain for the rest of her life. The prettiest girls had an edge; anyone homely or fat was almost certain to be snubbed. Poise and good manners also counted for something.'" For instance, debutantes were even trained to follow the conversational cues of their hostess, "to know by the turn of her head when to turn to speak to the man on the right or left of me." Sarah Churchill recalled that a maid kept a register of what she wore at each event, and "I would return from the hairdresser's to find the clothes I was to wear for the evening laid out on my bed." But among the girls, nothing mattered as much as social position. "'Family was essential,' said Lady Cathleen Eliot, who came out in the late 1930s. 'And to debs from good families, the rest simply didn't count. They would be ignored'" in what would be known as the *cut direct*: "'You know: somebody looks at you and you just look at them expressionless and your eyes move on, like that.'" The gatherings were social but also created the world of acknowledged hierarchy, acceptable marriage markets, and a network of political alliances.

Having cleared the hurdles of the Presentation and debutante balls, the upper class could relax to some degree and enjoy the other events that constituted The Season. One observer wrote, "it seemed as if 'a race of gods and goddesses descended from Olympus upon England in June and July.'" June saw a fortnight of celebrations between the Derby and Royal Ascot races. During July the elite would move to seaside resorts such as Brighton, followed by a foray down to Cowes for a week of yacht-racing. After Cowes, the gatherings moved to Scotland to begin shooting on the "Glorious 12th" of August—the opening of grouse season. In 1911, the *Tatler* magazine reported that $1.1 billion (2019 value) was spent on shooting alone. The speed with which servants could re-load guns allowed the group with Lord Burnham and George V to bag a record of nearly 4,000 grouse in one day in 1913. Later, the Henley Regatta and the Royal Academy's Summer Exhibition were accepted as sunset events of The Season, and the races at Goodwood in late August marked its conclusion. The elite then dispersed "to their country estates for hunting, Christmas and to await the coming of spring."

Although The Season was required attendance for people wishing to gain or maintain a place in society, other social delights were possible. Visits to great houses in the countryside were highly sought-after, though in the nineteenth century they had been limited primarily to estates that had their own rail stations. By the twentieth century, technology made visiting easier when in 1904 Charles Rolls and Frederick Henry Royce began production of their luxury cars. And, despite "the antiquated twelve-mile-an-hour speed limit in force until 1903," motor cars made even the most isolated estates accessible to the fortunate guest invited to stay and hunt, gossip, or dance. During this social whirl, there would be "Saturday to Monday" (not "weekend") trips to the country houses. Ladies could have twenty-five changes of clothing for such a stay that included teas, lawn sports, and elegant dinners. A competent hostess insured that "everything was as it should be: plenty of coal in the grate, fresh ribbons threaded through the hems of sheets, clean blotting paper, new pens, a full ink bottle and various sizes of writing paper at the desk; fresh flowers, perhaps corsages for the ladies (a speciality at the Sackville's Knole) and reading matter gauged to the occupants' tastes." Because each guest had a servant, an estate such as Chatsworth might have four hundred extra people to feed during a house party.

As one debutante later explained, "'House parties helped organize the upper class. They were a way of asserting the intimacy of a group of friends or of deciding whether to admit a new member... . They could be used to throw two people together for longer than just an evening... . They could even be used to test the social skills of a new girl... . Could she... stand up to scrutiny over a whole weekend? Were [her] clothes, manners, even sporting prowess up to scratch?'" Personal maids or the "upstairs servants took care of placing everyone's clothing carefully in drawers and closets." The country house party offered men the opportunity to hunt pheasant, grouse, and stag along with the promise of champagne and an elegant meal "in a luncheon tent (possibly provided with floorboards, windows and heating)." An invitation from a titled host still held more drawing power than that of the nouveau riche.

The country activities especially favored by the upper class were softened from their warlike antecedents and often involved horses. Polo, though preserving some elements of the cavalry charge, had its governing rules and always ended with whisky, comfortable dining, and jovial recounting of the action in the chukkers. Racing and breeding horses was not a business but a passion that drew people to rent houses near Newmarket and Epsom to cheer the horses of the Prince of Wales or Lord Rosebery. Point to point racing evolved from steeplechasing, the challenge to race from one church to the distant church steeple, leaping over walls, ditches, or any other obstacles in the way. Perhaps the most elegant equestrian event was fox-hunting with its hunting pinks (actually coats that were red in color and evolved from military uniforms), yelping hounds, and the clarion call of the horn. Enthusiasts "rode to hounds" five or six times a week. The Duke of Rutland's "family could always tell by the speed of morning prayers if [their chaplain] Mr. Knox were hunting that day or not." It was rumored that he "wore boots and spurs under his cassock." On the final day of her life, Lord Salisbury's grandmother – eighty-five and nearly blind – had herself lashed onto her horse and was accompanied by a groom who called as she approached a fence, "'Jump, dammit, my Lady, jump.'"

The large country houses had also offered opportunities for romantic assignations. One famously-repeated anecdote from the 1890s concerned Lord Charles Beresford who "let himself into what he believed was his mistress's bedroom and with a lusty cry of 'Cock-a-doodle-doo!' leaped into the bed only to discover that it was occupied by the Bishop of Chester and his wife.

To avoid such confusions, guests at Wentworth Woodhouse, a stately pile in Yorkshire, were given silver boxes containing personalized confetti, which they could sprinkle through the corridors to help find their way back to, or between, rooms. Some houses had name slots placed on the doors for ease of location. Another device was to have a bell "rung at 6 a.m. to warn lovers it was time to find their own rooms before the servants brought their tea."

Within this world there was a physical division between the upper class and the staffs where green baize covered the servant-side of serving doors "like the fabric on a snooker table, to muffle the unappealing smells and sounds of the lower orders." At the end of a visit, a house guest would acknowledge any valued assistance rendered by a servant by giving "vails." In a world that lacked the option of leaking gossip to tabloids, these tips could handsomely add to the income of house staff, which increased the desirability of entering service during the nineteenth century.

CHAPTER 6

A PANTHER AMONG NOBLES

Lord D'Abernon recorded meeting 23-year-old Jennie Jerome Churchill for the first time in 1877 in Dublin:

> The Viceroy was on a dais at the further end of the room surrounded by a brilliant staff, but eyes were not turned on him or his consort, but on a dark, lithe figure, standing somewhat apart and appearing to be of another texture to those around her, radiant, translucent, intense. A diamond star in her hair, her favorite ornament – its luster dimmed by the flashing glory of her eyes. More of the panther than of the woman in her look, but with a cultivated intelligence unknown to the jungle.

Jennie's beauty and "cultivated intelligence" carried her from her socially questionable American origins to the royal height of English aristocracy. She inherited some of her clear-eyed savvy insights from her father, Leonard Jerome. Leonard had gained his wealth during the Gilded Age of American entrepreneurship, dabbling in the railroad business with his friend Cornelius Vanderbilt, investing in the *New York Times*, and speculating in the stock market. He enjoyed yachting, thoroughbred racing, and hunts in the American West guided by Buffalo Bill Cody. His mansion in New York City had a ballroom with fountains that spouted champagne for his visitors. In short, his money made him feel he could do whatever he wanted. Though they never divorced, Leonard was entirely unfaithful to his wife Clarissa. One of his lovers was the world-renowned singer Jenny Lind, and Leonard had the temerity to persuade his wife to give that name to their second daughter.

Not surprisingly, then, when Jennie was thirteen, Clarissa moved with her three daughters to Paris and allowed Leonard's wealth to support them in an aristocratic lifestyle. The daughters acquired polish in the social graces and learned to navigate elite social circles, even becoming friends with the Empress Eugenie of France. Bismarck's invasion of France was the catalyst that sent the Jerome women to England in 1870.

Jennie Jerome's debut occurred in 1872 with her presentation to Prince Albert Edward and Princess Alexandra at Cowes, the small Isle of Wight village that swelled to prominence during the yacht races of The Season. From this time Jennie and the Prince of Wales were close, lifelong friends, probably even lovers. The next year at Cowes, Jennie met the twenty-three-year-old Randolph Churchill at a shipboard ball honoring the Tsar and Tsaress of Russia. He was slender, well-dressed, witty – and an English lord. She was classically modeled with a patrician nose and slightly pouting lips. Her dark hair and brows, her eyes, her gaze – a potent mix of challenge and invitation – created an air of smoky sexuality that would always excite men and draw them to her. She understood her power and used it effectively.

Three days later Randolph proposed marriage.

The Churchill family objections about the suitability of Leonard Jerome as a familial connection, as noted earlier, were muted on February 4 by Randolph's election to Parliament, cut short by the couple's marriage in Paris on April 15, and ended with the birth of Winston seven months later on November 30. After giving birth, Jennie returned to the social swirl that she envisioned as her future. She quickly became a favorite of the Prince of Wales who was very attracted to the wit and frankness of American women, and Jennie's beauty provided the added assurance that she would always be invited to his exclusive parties. It was possibly out of jealousy that Randolph may have shown Princess Alexandra the love letters from the Prince to Lady Aylesford. Regardless of the reason, the Randolph Churchills became *personae non gratae* and in 1876 sailed to Canada and from there across the United States. By the time they returned to England, Randolph's father had accepted an appointment as Viceroy to Ireland; Prime Minister Disraeli strongly suggested that Randolph accompany his father.

It was when Randolph Churchill was stationed in Ireland that many historians mark as the beginning of Jennie Churchill's affairs. This change in the Churchill marriage was representative of the accepted morality of the upper class at that time and a separate standard from the conventional Victorian morality espoused by Queen Victoria. Among families of a poorer economic class, a certain fidelity in marriage was expected because the family could not sustain the taking-on of any extramarital children. However, as William Manchester has observed, "In titled families it [Victorian morality] was meaningless. Only the legitimacy of the first patrician child counted" – "hence the shibboleth of never remarking on the paternal resemblance in an upper-class child." As Consuelo, Duchess of Marlborough acidly put it, she had done her marital duty when she had produced "an heir and a spare" and so was then free to do as she pleased.

The Churchill marriage was publicly successful: Randolph, as the second son of a Duke, had married a woman whose finances could support their lifestyle. Jennie had promptly produced a healthy heir, Winston. If, as many historians report, Randolph suffered from syphilis, their private life may have been more troubled. Regardless, while Randolph made trips to London reporting on the Irish situation, Jennie took up riding and came to love it with a passion. One of her favorite riding partners was John Strange Jocelyn, a handsome, dashing man who lived with his wife on a 9,000-acre family estate. It was said, "He was the kind of man who could climb up the drainpipe to a bedroom window, and did."

On February 4, 1880, Jennie gave birth in Dublin to a second son. The boy was always called Jack, but his proper name was John Strange Spencer-Churchill.

The Churchills finally ended their Irish exile and returned to England in 1880. Jennie used her powers as a popular campaigner for her husband. With her social assistance, within six years Randolph showed promise of being prime minister. During these exciting times, Randolph and Jennie, like most nobles, had little contact with their children. The sons had been reared by nannies, but Winston still idolized both of his parents and romanticized his closeness to them. In point of fact, though, he had had few real conversations with his father. Winston didn't even know whether his father attended Eton or Harrow. What little contact Randolph had with Winston generally ended in Randolph expressing a low opinion of his son's abilities: [you should be ashamed] of "'your slovenly happy-go-lucky harum scarum style of work.'"

Perhaps the most famous letter of Randolph to his son predicted that "if you cannot prevent yourself from leading the idle useless unprofitable life you have had during your schooldays & later months, you will become a mere social wastrel, one of the hundreds of the public school failures, and you will degenerate into a shabby unhappy & futile existence. If that is so you will have to bear all the blame for such misfortunes yourself." Despite this paternal judgment, Winston attempted to follow his father's political philosophies, rehabilitate his father's reputation, and achieve the same offices to which his father aspired.

Winston desperately sought the approval of his mother as well, once writing as a young student in France, "'Darling Mummy do attend to my letter. I am so wretched. Even now I weep. Please my darling Mummy be kind to your loving son. Don't let my silly letters make you angry. Let me at least think that you love me.'" Winston soon came to appreciate her persuasive powers and never hesitated to call on them. While he was a student at Harrow, the headmaster reported that Winston was slovenly, forgetful, careless, and unpunctual. Winston wrote his mother, "'You must stick up for me, because if you don't nobody else will.'" Jennie gradually worked to establish social and political connections for her son. Even though he was just a young boy at Harrow, she persuaded a Member of Parliament, Edward Carson, to visit him and explain some of the current political situation.

It was a medical problem that especially led Jennie to involve Winston in the lives of the influential men with whom she spent time. Winston had jumped off a thirty-foot bridge to avoid capture during a game of chase with his brother and cousin. While he recuperated from a ruptured spleen, his mother allowed him to join her dinner table "which, on various occasions, included three future prime ministers – Rosebery, Balfour, and Asquith – all of whom... would help shape Winston's future."

Like his father, Winston did not take his early studies seriously and often got in trouble. On a third attempt, Winston did pass the entrance exam for Sandhurst; but his low score meant that he would be a member of the Cavalry and so have to bear the expense of $28,000 per year plus the purchase of a charger, two hunters, and three polo ponies. His father was angry over the expense. After his father's death, Winston was implicated in a hazing scandal in which he and five other subalterns of the Four Hussars told a sixth man, Alan Cameron Bruce-Price, that he was not desired in the regiment. The case was settled for about $70,000 outside of court, but Winston wrote his mother that "'you must be the guardian of my young reputation.'" She would fill that role impressively for the rest of her life. She held tremendous power because, at age forty and a widow, her beauty and liveliness continued to make her much sought-after.

Jennie ultimately had nearly twenty lovers, among whom were included William Waldorf Astor, Austrian Count Charles Kinsky, Prince Albert Edward (later King Edward VII), and Bourke Cockran, the man who mentored Winston after Randolph Churchill's death. Jennie was lively—she could touch the mantelpiece with her foot when dancing the can-can—and practical—she knew when to resist lovers. Still, in July 1900 at age 45, she married George Cornwallis-West, who was her son Winston's age (26). According to a *New York Times* headline, "British Society [Was] Astonished." She divorced him thirteen years later. In 1918 at age 64 she married Montague Porch who was three years younger than Winston.

During World War I for reasons of personal safety, the government would not give her leave to travel with her new husband to the then-dangerous country of Nigeria, so she stayed and spent time in the new nightclubs. Lady Diana Cooper recalled the night when her neighborhood was hit in a zeppelin raid. Amid the panic and moans of the wounded, a tipsy Jennie Churchill (Porch) and Maud Cunard stopped by for a drink.

Her adventures abruptly ended though after a visit to Rome. In May 1921 she was visiting Lady Frances Horner at Mells Manor in Somerset. Winston's personal secretary, Eddie Marsh, once observed about Jennie that "'Life didn't begin for her on a basis of less than forty pairs of shoes'" so, ironically, the accident involved shoes. She was preparing to go to a tea party and hurried down the stairs in a pair of new shoes. Three steps from the landing, she fell and broke her left leg just above the ankle. After a few days, gangrene set in and the doctors recommended amputation: "Jennie calmly said she would learn 'to put my best foot forward' and added: 'Be sure you cut high enough.'" They amputated the leg above the knee, and she rested comfortably at home. Then, two weeks later the femoral artery in her left thigh hemorrhaged and she died on June 29, 1921, at age 67 with her sons Jack and Winston at her side. Her sons were devastated.

Jennie had had a profound effect on many men, but particularly upon her son Winston. As Prime Minister, Winston would, for reasons both emotional and political, remind the 32nd US President Franklin Delano Roosevelt and the American Congress of his American blood.

CHAPTER 7

RULE, BRITANNIA: EMPIRE, AMBITION, AND RUPTURE

In 1898, a young American Lieutenant Colonel, eyes squinting against the clouds of acrid gunpowder hanging in the air, roared up the San Juan Heights of Cuba and into fame, followed by a riotous gang of Rough Riders. Theodore Roosevelt would later capture the office of President of the United States as well. In the meantime, he was supporting Cuba's third attempt to gain independence from Spain. The conflict was murderous, had lasted years, and would ultimately succeed after killing a quarter of the island's population. Three years earlier in the conflict, a kindred spirit from England read the Cuban news releases and, similarly, could hardly wait to risk his life amid the bloody struggle. Second Lieutenant Winston Churchill wrote Jennie Jerome Churchill:

> My dearest Mamma,
>
> I daresay you will find the content of this letter somewhat startling. The fact is that I have decided to go with a great friend of mine, one of the subalterns in the regiment, to American and the W. Indies... We shall go to New York & after a stay there move in a steamer to the W. Indies - to Havana where all the Government troops are collecting to go up country and suppress the revolt that is still simmering on.

Jennie replied as though agreeing to a boyish lark, "I understand all right – & of course darling it is natural that you shd want to travel & I won't throw cold water on yr little plans."

Winston may well have bristled at those last words because hundreds of young men like him and Roosevelt were intoxicated with a fiery battle fever concocted from the imperial ambitions and histories of their countries – and they did not want to miss the excitement. As a boy, Winston had maneuvered his thousand toy soldiers to recapitulate the exact battle movements of Blenheim and Waterloo. As a young man, he and other subalterns in India galloped recklessly in polo chukkers to practice for cavalry charges. Aristocratic English officers took leave and paid their own expenses so as not to miss a pop-up war. Sometimes they lead military charges "brandishing only cigars or swagger sticks." As early as 1817 John Wilson had proudly declared that "the sun never sets upon the Union Jack." These aristocrats saw the British Empire as the resplendent embodiment of the nation's greatness and the natural extension of their family preserve. No young noble could resist being part of such glory.

The rebellion in Cuba came at an especially timely moment for Churchill. Having completed his training at Sandhurst, he had ten weeks of leave before reporting for duty in India with the 4th Queen's Own Hussars. Eager to get into the Cuban fray, he contacted his father's old publisher and secured an agreement to send dispatches that would cover his expenses. He then contacted his mother's friends, Ambassador to Spain Drummond Wolff and the Commander in Chief of the Army Lord Wolseley, who provided him with full briefings and military maps – the Churchill name extracting an extraordinary extension of courtesy to so junior an officer. He and a friend then sailed to New York where they were met by another of Jennie's lovers, Bourke Cockran, who secured a private train compartment for their journey to Key West. From there they sailed on the steamer *Olivette* to Cuba where Churchill would blissfully find himself under fire, promote his career by filing five reports for *The Daily Graphic*, and acquire a lifelong passion for Cuban cigars.

The British Empire would provide him with adventures and fame to lift him to the forefront of English public life.

***

The British Empire had derived some of its passion and motivating force from an entirely unexpected source: the clash of Victorian scientific theory and religious philosophy. Charles Darwin's theory of evolution hit Victorian society like an explosion because his *Origin of Species* specifically denied that there was a divine hand in creation. Opponents gasped, turned in fear and anger to a defense of Christianity, and came to regard all scientific proposals with suspicion. Rigidity and naiveté of belief became a hallmark of conventional Victorian morality, an "earnestness" mocked by Oscar Wilde's *The Importance of Being Earnest* (1895).

With varying degrees of compassion but an emphatic conviction of following God's will, men and women took to the mission fields to spread Christianity to the benighted heathen. British missionaries traveled to the farthest reaches of Africa, South America, and Asia in their moral imperative. Ironically, scientific breakthroughs such as Jose Lister's discovery of antiseptics and the development of the smallpox vaccine preserved the health of Victorian missionaries as they sought to spread their faith into subtropical continents.

The case of the Scottish missionary David Livingstone suggests how glamor came to be associated with the British incursions into exotic locales. Although he never successfully converted many Africans, David Livingstone became a national hero, though not particularly for his role as a medical missionary. Livingstone's goal in his travels was to aid other missionaries by mapping the river systems and cataloging the resources of the continent. In particular, he developed an obsession with discovering the origins of the Nile. He courageously extended the map of Africa, fought the ravages of malaria, and broke his arm while defending a village's sheep against a marauding lion. His rise to fame occurred because he lost contact with the outside world for six years, prompting the *New York Herald* to send Henry Morton Stanley to locate him. The search became a source of international interest and raised Livingstone's mission to a celebrated height. In 1871 on the shores of Lake Tanganyika, Stanley supposedly greeted the only white man within hundreds of miles with the now-famous words, "Dr. Livingstone, I presume?"

Livingstone's missionary passion coincided with and supported Britain's political will to expand the Empire. When he discovered the most dramatic waterfalls in Africa, Livingstone renamed them for Queen Victoria. His mapping of rivers and resources proved useful to merchants and soldiers more than missionaries. A line was crossed when the mission of religious conversion of heathen became blurred with the mission of military domination of their countries. As Rudyard Kipling's poem later phrased it, it was "The White Man's Burden" (1899) to enlighten—in fact, dominate – the developing world. *Being Christian* had become linked with *being British*.

As events evolved, a pattern of incursion developed: Missionaries-Merchants-Military. The missionaries became dependent upon merchants who supplied distant outposts; and those merchants came to see and covet the wealth of export markets and of raw materials available in these undeveloped countries. Soon the British military came to protect the economic interests of the Empire. By 1839, Britain forced Indian opium trade onto China, essentially for the benefit of the East India Company, a company which actually ruled India from 1757-1858. In 1858 India became "the Jewel in the Crown" of Queen Victoria. Aristocrats ranging from Lord Canning to 1st Marquess George Curzon vied to become governor-general of the British Raj for the political prestige and economic windfall it offered. By 1875 Britain was a major shareholder in the Suez Canal controlling the critical East-West route to India and China. Administrators like Bertie Mitford provided the final seal upon the Empire's acquisitions by incorporating their management into the official bureaucracy of the British government.

The reach and grandeur of the British Empire at its height were unparalleled in the history of the world. The genuine pride in the world-embracing influence of the Empire was later captured in Edward Elgar's "Pomp and Circumstance":

Land of hope and glory, mother of the free,
How shall we extol thee, who art born of thee?
Wider still and wider shall thy bounds be set;
God who made thee mighty, make thee mightier yet;
God who made thee mighty, make thee mightier yet!

In 1896 when Winston Churchill finally reported for his first military tour of duty in India, he entered a land that was exotic and luxurious for a young English officer. As a member of the 4th Hussars, he was paid little but could still afford a boy to take care of his uniforms, a groom for his ponies, a cook, housekeeper, and workers to carry water and maintain the garden he shared with other subalterns. Days consisted of 90 minutes of drills and parades in the morning and then leisure time until 5 p.m. when, in the cool of the evening, the young men engaged in polo, "the pivot around which the life of all cavalry officers in India centred."

Under his terms of duty in India—what little they were—Churchill was granted five month's leave per year, which made possible his "little plans" to go to Cuba in 1895. Cuba would produce a life-altering change of purpose and ambition in Churchill. He began a course of self-education, peppering his mother with requests to ship him books he had neglected while in school. Like his father, he memorized significant literary passages that he would practice aloud until he could call them to mind without hesitation. With a newly-awakened sense of imperial ambition, he developed an absolute passion to make a name for himself and follow in his father's footsteps as a Member of Parliament and leader of the nation.

In 1897 while Churchill was home on leave from India, done with Cuba, and enjoying The Season, the British garrison in Malakand in the northwest region of India came under siege. When Churchill heard of it, he begged General Sir Bindon Blood to allow him to join the relief force. Blood agreed that he could come, but only as an imbedded correspondent in the relief force. Churchill was ecstatic: he made the 2,000-mile trip back to India in five days. Not surprisingly, along with the other troops, Winston came under hot fire and immediately abandoned his correspondent role and fought. The siege was lifted successfully, and Winston wrote up his account that was published as *The Story of the Malakand Field Force: An Episode of Frontier War*. The book was a riveting read, and even Jennie's love, the Prince of Wales congratulated him on his entrance into national awareness. On the other hand, his regiment and officers disliked him for being such a "self-advertiser" and a presumptuous know-it-all for criticizing the general's conduct of the campaign. This would not be the last time these criticisms were lodged against him.

Churchill was undeterred. In 1898 he called on several social connections so he could be part of the Empire's revenge for the death of General Charles Gordon at Khartoum. In 1885 Gordon and his men had been butchered by dervishes of the Mahdi in the Sudan. Since that time a new Khalifa had sought to lead a jihad to reform the Moslem world. His saber-rattling provided the English with an excuse to go into the Sudan to avenge Gordon and then, conveniently, to push the French out of the Nile River Valley.

Churchill, now twenty-three and a mere lieutenant, blithely asked the Commander-in-Chief, Sir Herbert Kitchener, for permission to join the expedition. Kitchener, angered by the presumption demonstrated in the Malakand book, refused. Undaunted, Winston got Jennie to appeal to the Prince of Wales; Kitchener still refused. With Winston's encouragement, Jennie decided to go to Egypt to petition Kitchener; he still refused. Finally, Winston brazenly appealed to the Prime Minister, Lord Salisbury, who promised to help.

The time frame was so immediate that Winston went to the Private Secretary, Sir McDonnell, "who interrupted his dinner plans to handle the matter."

Churchill left his regiment in India and took a steamer from Bangalore to Marseilles and then on to Cairo. At about 6 a.m. on Friday, September 2, the Battle of Omdurman began, the British artillery quickly decimating 11,000 dervishes. At one point Kitchener kept repeating, "'Cease fire! Cease Fire! Cease fire! Oh, what a dreadful waste of ammunition!'" Churchill himself participated in perhaps the last successful cavalry charge in British history, and he thought it "magnificent": "'I raised my voice and helmet in honour of that persevering British people who, often affronted, usually get their own way in the end.'" If he had not been so before, he was now a confirmed believer in the Empire. His record of the battle again helped his career trajectory as well. As was true with his account of the Malakand siege, Churchill's coverage of the fighting was gripping, eloquent, and earned him more name recognition, even as his rising prominence irked his military colleagues.

The fourth and final adventure of young imperial Churchill occurred the next year, 1899. It was the episode that finally gained for him the international fame which he desired so passionately: The Boer Wars. The Boer Wars were sometimes called the Khaki Wars because these were the first conflicts in which the British had shed their traditional red uniforms for the safer, more functional properties of khaki. The conflict had its origins in the Conference of Berlin (1884-1885) that partitioned Africa among European powers without inviting any Africans to participate in the decisions. At first England had been satisfied with the South African colonies Natal and Cape Colony. Then gold and diamonds were discovered in the nearby Boer colonies of the Transvaal and the Orange Free State. To many imperialists like Cecil Rhodes, diamonds were "crystallised power." To an Empire based on the gold standard, the lure was irresistible.

Winston, now out of the military, sought again to report on battles. He and his valet set sail for Cape Town in October, three days after the first shots were fired. A friend from India days, Captain Aylmer Haldane, invited Winston to travel on a train with troops who were to explore the Boer lines. Predictably, the Boers piled rocks on the tracks, wrecked the train, and killed or captured the survivors. Churchill took up arms and bravely resisted the attack until all further efforts were futile. Churchill, now captured, walked the sixty-mile trek to Elandslaagte and then was transported by train to the prisoner-of-war camp in Pretoria.

The imprisonment angered and depressed him. He wrote Transvaal authorities saying he had been a non-combatant – which was not true, a fact confirmed in the press by reporters who had been present and reported on his fighting. He wrote his mother and the Prince of Wales, but they could not help. Meanwhile Haldane and another soldier conceived a plan of escape by climbing from a latrine over a remote wall. Churchill insisted on joining them. He, in fact, was able to escape successfully using their plan, but Haldane and Brockie could not find a safe opportunity. With little food, no map, and no knowledge of the language Africaans, Churchill began his escape strategy by boldly strolling through Pretoria. There he hopped on a train and rode out of the city. After days of struggle and wandering, he desperately approached a house and had the good fortune to discover the only British house for twenty miles. They hid him for three nights in a mine. Meanwhile, the British press had gotten news of the escape and publicized his likely punishment of facing a firing squad if captured again, and the public anxiously sought news of his progress.

His saviors conceived the plan of smuggling Churchill in a consignment of wool bales. One man, Charles Burnham, risked his life to ride the train and look out for Churchill's progress. When he finally passed into safe Portuguese East Africa, Winston strode to the British Consulate, and shouted, "'I am Winston Bloody Churchill! Come down here at once.'" His escape was a news sensation. A handsome young aristocrat whose pluck had won him freedom, Churchill was a full-fledged hero in England.

It would be no surprise that he immediately sought to follow his father's path into politics and even less surprising that his first political speech would show his love of the Empire:

> We should show by our actions that the vigour and vitality of our race is unimpaired and that our determination is to uphold the Empire that we have inherited from our fathers as Englishmen, that our flag shall fly high upon the sea, our voice be heard in the councils of Europe, our Sovereign be supported by the love of her subjects. Then we shall continue to pursue that course marked out for us by an all-wise hand and carry out our mission of bearing peace, civilisation and good government to the uttermost ends of the earth.

***

The sword of Empire cut both ways. For some men like Bertie Mitford, their tour of duty in the foreign service offered possible entrée into the seats of political power and elite society upon their return to England. However, the business ventures of the British Empire began to destabilize the importance of inherited lands at home. Initially, as members of the first industrialized nation in the world, the British upper class had advantages of investment capital, military might, and political will. Aristocrat-owned mines produced tons of coal to fire the boilers of steam locomotives and iron paddle-steamers that hauled industrial loads and passengers eastward to the Orient and southward to the Mediterranean and Africa. However, men outside of the upper-class social circles began to acquire immense wealth that matched or surpassed the inherited wealth. For example, enterprising men of the middle class had traveled to South Africa, making their fortunes with the discovery and sale of gold and diamonds. These "Randlords"—a term coined by their currency – returned to England with fabulous wealth and established themselves in great houses and homes throughout the country. As the Empire expanded, non-nobles made valuable contributions to the crown by creating wealth in banking, textiles, steel, beer, chemical manufacture, shipping and ship-building, armaments, and later motor cars. The crown sometimes rewarded them with titles; they rewarded themselves with—among other things – great country houses.

As Clive Aslet observed, "country-house building was quite an accurate index of the economy"; and in the period 1890 to 1939, country houses were an indicator of the degree to which New Wealth was attempting to identify itself with Old Wealth. Beer made possible the construction of Polesden Lacy, and banking provided the financial basis for Rodmarton Manor. Shipping and shipbuilding were the basis for Pangbourne Towers while armaments made possible Besford Court. Chemical and armaments funded the construction of Wretham Hall while steel-maker Andrew Carnegie had Skibo Castle remodeled on a massive scale. Diamonds allowed Cecil Rhodes to buy Dalham Hall and Julius Wernher to purchase Luton. Soap merchant Joseph Watson bought Compton Verney. Edward Guinness, who ran the largest brewery in the world, was raised to the rank of Earl of Iveagh. He was able to purchase Elveden, an estate in Suffolk, where the household employed sixteen gamekeepers, nine underkeepers, twenty-eight warreners (for culling rabbits), and where visitors shot over a hundred thousand birds every year. These hunting possibilities were attractive to the upper class, even though the title of the owner was newly minted. Given the wealth and country houses of these entrepreneurs, it became difficult for the untrained eye to determine which was authentic Old Wealth and which the imitation.

Like titled families, the newly wealthy also copied the aristocratic impulse to re-shape the land. Even Americans such as William Randolph Hearst and William Waldorf Astor felt that they could purchase this authenticity – and its attendant condescension – through their purchases of country houses. Millionaire William Waldorf Astor built tall walls around the park at Cliveden to keep the public from using the lake for boating. At his other estate, Hever Castle, he had 800 men with six steam diggers lay seven miles of railway line, dig a 35-acre lake, build a "Tudor Village" to house his guests, and wall off that lake as well. Wags would suggest that his real middle name was "Walled-Off."

These parvenus could even afford to employ the same architects and landscape designers who served the upper class. One of the most sought-after architects during this age of elegant construction was Sir Edwin Lutyens who collaborated with plantswoman and gardener Gertrude Jekyll to develop a vocabulary of house and garden design. The magazine *Country Life*, in presenting pages of their work, established itself—and Lutyens and Jekyll—as arbiters of style. A Lutyens garden could be readily identified by its intricately paved and patterned paths, the use of stone and brick, and his method of establishing vistas that connected with the house. In speaking to the Architectural Association in April 1908, Lutyens affirmed that "A garden scheme should have a backbone—a central ideal beautifully phrased." Because "The true adornment of a garden lies surely in its flowers and plants," the elite looked to Jekyll to provide "a careful crescendo of effect." Architect Edwin Lutyens not only designed the *Country Life* offices at Covent Garden but also reflected in much of his house design and remodeling the values of William Morris and the Arts and Crafts movement. Edwardian gardens owe much to this sense of nostalgia and to the notion of the garden as an extension of the house itself. In the 1930s Vita Sackville-West and her husband Harold Nicolson would design separate gardens as "rooms" at their home Sissinghurst, a new standard for landscape gardening at great estates.

Yet even at the turn of the century, political and economic cracks were appearing within the seamlines of the upper-class way of life. Their great country houses would be the canaries in the mine. Country houses were built by one of two types of owner: those who wanted a house with modern conveniences and who saw "land ownership as a means to social advance. The other type of owner wanted a country house either because the country [house] embodied a [world] they saw disappearing" or wanted to avoid the nouveau riche. In his excellent study *The Last Country Houses,* architectural historian Clive Aslet described the economic problem: "Born late in the evolutionary chain, they [these country houses] were nevertheless great mammoths of domestic architecture and were frequently unable to adapt to the change in habitat that followed the two World Wars. Inflexible in their service arrangements, they grazed in a savannah of cheap labour and cheap fuel, they baked beneath a sky in which the filmy clouds of income tax and death duties had only just begun to appear."

To a great degree, the country estates' demise became a physical symptom of the financial limitations of the titled rich. Indeed, the economic problems of the country estates were symptomatic of larger social changes arising within the Empire. Fissures in the absolute dominance of the English upper class appeared when the traditional understandings and alliances broke down. For the system to stay intact, the rules had to matter. Marital infidelities needed to be discreet. Nobles had to support their social class. The upper class was destined to rule. Old Wealth signified. The smallest of fault lines, thought the nobles, would lead to the breaching of the structure, the collapse of their world.

They were right.

CHAPTER 8

THE UNWINDING OF PRIVILEGE: LLOYD GEORGE, KING EDWARD VII, AND TEASING THE GOLDFISH

"Was this the face that launched a thousand ships?" was a game that Winston Churchill and his private secretary Eddie Marsh played at debutante parties. Using the legendary beauty of Helen of Troy as their standard, they would nonchalantly stand beside the dance floor surveying the young women and allotting to each face a tally of ships. Their judgments were so rigorous that the glamorous Diana Manners (later Lady Cooper) was one of only two women awarded a full armada of one thousand. In all of their hours of gaming, only one other young woman would match that total: the Honourable Clementine Hozier.

Clementine—or Clemmie as she was known familiarly—was universally regarded as a charming young woman. Her classic features were complemented by large wide-set eyes, hazel-green in color, and luxurious ash-brown hair. Violet Asquith, the Prime Minister's daughter, judged that Clementine had "'a face of classical perfection'" and a profile like "'the prow of a Greek ship.'" Her attractive looks were matched by high spirits and an intelligent mind. In 1904 when Clementine was first introduced to him, Churchill had simply stared and scarcely spoken a word to her. By age twenty-three, she had studied at the Sorbonne, chosen a left-of-Liberal political stance for herself, and already reconsidered and broken two engagements. Her sister Nellie suggested "that a file of 'Proposals to Clementine' should be kept, with the headings: 'Discussed,' 'Answered,' and 'Pending Decision.'" This "Helen" would not settle for a stare or an Hellenic comparison.

Clementine's aristocratic credentials were strong. Her maternal grandparents, the Olgivys of the House of Airlie, had a long notable lineage in Scotland tracing back to the fifteenth century. Her mother Blanche, eldest daughter of the 10th Earl of Airlie, was known affectionately by family and friends as "Natty." Blanche's debut and whirlwind social life brought the 26-year-old to marry 40-year-old Sir Henry Montague Hozier. In time the Hoziers became the parents of four children. To outward appearances, the marriage was social perfection. In reality, both husband and wife were serially unfaithful to each other, the marriage managing to stumble on for some years only because all parties remained discreet.

A cardinal rule of upper-class social behavior was that love affairs were acceptable so long as they remained discreet. Blanche pushed the boundaries too far. Her extramarital love life was so extensive that there has always been debate as to the paternity of her children. Sir Henry and Lady Blanche Hozier may have been officially recorded as Clementine's parents, but the identity of her biological father was never determined. Blanche's granddaughter Mary Churchill Soames thought the father was Captain William George "Bay" Middleton. Blanche herself told Lady Londonderry that Clementine's father was Blanche's brother-in-law, Algernon "Bertie" Freeman-Mitford, 1st Baron Redesdale. If that were the case, it was a complex twist of family history that later found Clementine Hozier's nephew Esmond Romilly eloping to the Spanish Civil War with Bertie Mitford's granddaughter Jessica. Regardless, no one believed Clementine Hozier's father was Sir Henry Hozier.

Matters came to a head in 1891 when Sir Henry actually caught Blanche with a lover and threatened divorce. The Hoziers separated. Lady Blanche battled Sir Henry for financial support and managed to see that her children received the benefits of travel abroad and study in France. For the rest of her life, though, Blanche would remain on the distant margins of the social class that judged her a public disgrace.

Fortunately, her parents' publicly-aired affairs did not fatally damage Clementine's prospects. On September 12, 1908, three weeks after their official engagement, she and Winston married at St. Margaret's, Westminster, the London church in which David and Sydney Mitford had been married four years previously. By this time Winston had achieved some national prominence, and so the wedding was covered extensively by the press. Jennie Churchill's devoted friend King Edward sent Winston a gold-topped walking stick. Clementine dazzled in a gown of white satin and a veil of tulle accented by fresh orange blossoms. It was a portent of life ahead that, following the service, Clementine found Winston in the church vestry discussing politics with Chancellor of the Exchequer Lloyd George. In the nine years since his Boer War escape, Churchill had parleyed his fame into a seat in Parliament and the position of Colonial Under-Secretary.

Governing had been the historical purview of the English upper class; and it remained a world where class, family, and politics intertwined. Winston Churchill was by birth and temperament a Tory—a conservative who believed that the upper class ruled because of its ability, taste, and breeding. His family's position in that society had already opened many doors for him into a world of fame and governance: so, naturally, he first stood for office as a Tory. His restive ambition chafed, however, when after four years he had failed to advance in the political ranks. In a move solely dictated by ambition, Winston switched parties to become a Liberal. One can scarcely overstate the shock and betrayal felt by his family and social class. His change in alliance constituted opposition to the protections and privileges that the elite had enjoyed for centuries. He showed himself to be a traitor to his family and friends at a time when the political foundations were crumbling underneath them.

Four economic and political reasons contributed to the dismantling of the aristocratic hegemony at this time. First, the English agricultural system became depressed in the 1870s, in part because of competition from the cheap imported goods arriving from a burgeoning American farm system. Second, the middle class did not own land, but they did now own shops and small businesses. Their new-found financial clout forced Parliament to pay attention to their business concerns, especially regarding tax laws that heretofore favored the gentry. Third, the Third Reform Act of 1884-85 extended suffrage and redistributed seats based upon population rather than on historical title. This broader voting franchise threatened the power of the House of Lords. Fourth, some new peers who had gained their titles through industry rather than inheritance sought to advance the causes of entrepreneurs. Their support of business worked also against the traditional interests of the House of Lords.

Many historians regard Lloyd George's People's Budget of 1909 as the death knell of the aristocracy's political dominance. Lloyd George proposed to cope with funding deficits in Old Age Pensions and naval construction with – among other things – a new supertax on incomes over $640,000 (2019 value), a measure affecting 11,500 people. He also proposed a tax on undeveloped land. Finally, he proposed what the nobles derisively called "death duties" on inherited wealth, which certainly targeted the great estates. Lloyd George contended that "'A fully-equipped duke…costs as much to keep up as two dreadnoughts; and dukes are just as great a terror and they last longer.'" By any objective assessment, this budget was designed with the expressed intent of redistributing wealth among the British public. Freshly-minted Liberal Winston Churchill concluded that the budget was a necessary choosing of representative government over aristocratic rule.

Though by contemporary standards, the size of the supertax was not excessive and was repealed in 1920, the "Great landowners publicly paraded their new-found poverty, and made it plain that others would suffer, too." Churchill wryly joked that attacking the Dukes was "poor sport—almost like teasing goldfish. These ornamental creatures blunder on[to] every hook they see… ." Winston's exasperated ducal cousin "Sunny" Marlborough told Winston's wife, "'Please, Clemmie, would you mind not writing to that horrible little man [Lloyd George] on Blenheim writing paper.'"

Turncoat Churchill was widely attacked as "the grandson of one duke, the nephew of another, and the cousin of a third… who owed every advantage he possessed to his ducal and aristocratic connections." Lord Beaufort wanted to set hounds on all of the Liberals; Lord Buccleuch petulantly cancelled his subscription to a football club. However, the patrician complaints did not air well with the public, and Lloyd George seized his advantage. In September 1909 during a speech at Newcastle, he excoriated the lords who were howling because of their increased taxes. How, he asked, could "'five hundred. . . ordinary men, chosen accidentally from among the unemployed' override 'the judgment of millions of people who are engaged in the industry which makes the wealth of the country?'"

Historically, the House of Lords had not vetoed government budgets; in November 1909, against precedent, they did. Public outcry, new elections, and pressure came to bear upon King Edward VII. The pressure became so great that Edward secretly agreed that he would be prepared to flood the House of Lords with newly created peers in order to ensure that the Parliament Bill could be passed. Under such a threat, the Lords capitulated and, essentially, lost their power to veto budget items. This single change would forever weaken the power of the Lords.

The new tax code for undeveloped land made the old scale of land ownership financially prohibitive for most titled families, forcing the sale of ancestral land. The reduction in acreage of many country estates, immense by modern standards, was breathtaking. By 1920, the Duke of Rutland was forced to sell 27,000 acres in Leicestershire and Derbyshire. Within the hundred years between 1876 to 1976, the estates of the Dukes of Northumberland would be forced to reduce their lands from 186,379 to 105,000 acres; and the estates of the Dukes of Devonshire reduced from 132,996 to 56,000 acres. During that same period the estates of Bertie Mitford and his heirs shrank from a modest 30,247 acres to a humbling 1,000 acres.

To the nobility in 1909 these changes were especially painful and mystifying because they extended into the social fabric of their class. King Edward VII could not foresee the consequences of his threat to flood the House of Lords, nor could he see his role as a pivotal figure in fracturing the social codes of the upper class.

Because of Queen Victoria's longevity, Edward had been a king-in-waiting for nearly sixty of his sixty-eight years. Excluded by his mother from political power, the Prince spent his life in a leisured existence. Most consistently, the Prince chose his friends among those whose finances allowed them to entertain the Prince in the ways he most enjoyed. Traditionally, the preference of a Prince had been conferred among the titled; now the royal cachet included anyone who could entertain him to perfection. Some of the Prince's friends "were not merely new, but so conspicuously *arriviste* that Society shuddered to read the [royal] court circular."

In addition, the Prince eschewed any rules that sought to constrain him. In 1870 he became the first Prince of Wales in history forced to appear at a public divorce proceeding because of his involvement with Mrs. Harriet Mordaunt. His lovers were numerous, and he "usually made his royal conquests in a private dining room above a fashionable restaurant; one paneled wall swung down at the touch of a button, exposing a double bed." He especially favored the American heiresses who had the money and liveliness to attend well to his interests. Jennie Churchill had been especially astute at judging "the level of his impatience and boredom, the danger point of his anger, and what to do about them."

Further, Edward did not care whether he offended any peer of the realm. In 1899 as Prince Edward, he snubbed the 80-year-old Duke of Richmond because the Duke would not include in the party two of the Prince's favorite lovers. He instead stayed at nearby Moulton Paddocks because "it had a croquet lawn, excellent partridge shooting" and a cook who prepared Edward's favorite meals.

When he was finally crowned on August 9, 1902, Edward VII sought the Modern Age. He brought modern plumbing, a telephone system, dancing, and cigarettes to Buckingham Palace. Friends vied to take him to horse races, motoring, shooting, gambling. They attended to his smallest desires, seeking to entertain with cards, gourmet food, music, and beautiful ladies. Though his official residence was now Buckingham Palace, his group of worldly friends were still called the "Marlborough House Set" after his personal London home. He traveled with two valets and changed clothes at least six times a day. When, as King, he visited Kylemore Abbey in Ireland in 1904, "the railroad station was enlarged and elaborately decorated with red carpets and masses of flowers"; the total cost of the visit was estimated to be $150,000.

An example of an untitled friend who attended to Edward's whims and gained entrée into the upper class despite his origins was Alfred de Rothschild. Alfred was the fabulously wealthy son of Jewish banker Lionel de Rothschild who had advanced $400 million (2019 value) to the British government to purchase 44 per cent of the Suez Canal shares from the Khedive of Egypt. Alfred's wealth meant that he could have every luxury he desired and ignore practically every social rule. He had a child out of wedlock with Mrs. Marie Boyer Wombell; and when the daughter came of age, Edward's approval of Alfred shielded illegitimate daughter Almina so she could be accepted as the bride of the cash-strapped Earl of Carnarvon.

Rothschild persuaded Edward to favor the Carnarvons with a visit at their country house Highclere Castle and guided Almina in every aspect of her preparations. Almina had a large bed constructed to support Edward's tremendous size; she redecorated the house; she knew every detail of his preferences, even to the pleasure he took in having lobster salad at tea. For this three-day visit, the Rothschild wealth spent nearly $535,000 (2019 value). The Rothschild wealth easily lured Edward to ignore upper-class sensibilities regarding title and privilege. Under Edward's aegis, money was now "admired with a frankness which mid-Victorians would have called vulgar."

Edward had spent most of his life as a heavy smoker, smoking a dozen cigars and nearly two dozen cigarettes a day. Combined with his corpulence, he developed bouts of bronchitis and eventually suffered a series of heart attacks. When he died on May 6, 1910, Edward's last reported words were pleasure at knowing his horse *Witch of the Air* had won at the Kempton Park races that day. It was a measure of his wife Alexandra's patience that she summoned his last mistress, the Honorable Mrs. George Keppel, to his deathbed.

By the end of Edward's rule, the upper class had felt that its right to govern, its social rules, and its wealth were unraveling in the new world of the twentieth century. Then began the most horrific of family arguments among Queen Victoria's grandchildren: World War I. Victoria's heirs sat on the thrones of Germany, Russia, Greece, Romania, Spain, Norway, and Britain; yet, their family and social ties would not constrain them from a breathtaking family brawl framing a nationalist desire to dominate Europe. The embattled English nobles grasped this conflict as a moment of opportunity: the chance to prove their worth by leading troops to glorious victory. Then perhaps the taxation battles would be put to rest, the bewildering agitations by workers forgotten, and all of life return to its traditional patterns.

CHAPTER 9

WORLD WAR I:
QUEST FOR GLORY

If I should die, think only this of me:
That there's some corner of a foreign field
That is forever England.

"The Soldier" by Rupert Brooke, 1915
Died of sepsis during World War I, aged 27

Tsar Nicholas of Russia and Kaiser Wilhelm II of Germany were cousins of King Edward VII and of his son-successor King George V. They had shared holidays together and visits with their grandmother Victoria: she would have expected them all to behave properly. They did not. Queen Victoria's eldest grandchild, Wilhelm II of Germany, had long seethed over the range and power of the Empire ruled by his English cousins. Near the end of his grandmother's reign, he had quietly begun a build-up of the German navy with an eye towards challenging the British dominance on the high seas. Britain made alliances with France (1904) and Russia (1907) to counter this saber-rattling. Ultimately multiple European accords were put to the test when on July 28, 1914, the heir to the Austrian throne was assassinated in Bosnia by a young Serbian nationalist. Austria, encouraged by Germany, went to war with Serbia. Serbia was in turn supported by Russia. Four days after the assassination, Germany declared war on Russia; and four days after that, Britain supported its ally and entered the war.

Like linked Alpiners scaling a cliff and suddenly tangled in a byzantine system of alliances, Europe had lurched and then plunged into the abyss of the first world-wide war. By July 17, 1917, King George V had obliterated his family ties to Germany by changing the name of the British Royal Family from the Germanic name of *Saxe-Coburg and Gotha* to the *House of Windsor*. The 1918 British Victory Medal would call this "The Great War For Civilisation," but the cost would be staggering. On Monday, August 3, 1914, Sir Edward Grey famously remarked, "'The lamps are going out all over Europe; we shall not see them lit again in our lifetime." He could not have foreseen that the catastrophic collision between an antiquated horse-based military model and a newly-mechanized war machine would cause the destruction of 12 million conscripted horses and mules. He could not have known the carnage that trench warfare, poison gas, and a highly mechanized war would wreak. He could not have envisioned the cultural changes that would alter the world irrevocably. Yet, at this last moment in August when Britain clung to its final day of peace, Grey had a presentiment that the web of political alliances would extinguish the light of humanity's better angels. When the war ended four years later, it would have caused the deaths of over 17 million people.

Meanwhile, those without Grey's presentiment greeted the prospect of war, for it suddenly pushed aside bewildering social issues in a general move to defend Civilization—in particular, Britain – against German imperialism. Patriotic zeal had been stirred to a rolling boil in recent years by writers like Rudyard Kipling who early fretted about the German naval buildup. Kipling complained loudly that his fellow Britons were "camping comfortably on the raw edge of a volcano." He almost single-handedly established a fashion of mocking the Germans as 'Huns' or 'Goths'" and shared the opinion of "many influential Britons [who] expected that a brisk campaign in Europe would be a welcome spine-stiffener for a country in danger of going soft."

When the dominoes fell against each other, Britons, no longer polarized by class and economic issues, volunteered in droves. In 1914 alone 1,186,351 British citizens from throughout the Empire joined up, overwhelming army enlistment and training capabilities. The zeal was so great that in many cases, all the young men from a particular village or district would join together in "pals" battalions. No one foresaw poison gas, trench rot, or death from hanging on the barbed wire of "No Man's Land." No one could foresee that mechanized warfare would have the devastating effect of killing all of a village's younger male generation with a single bomb blast.

The English upper class especially approached the war with high expectations. In the year 1914 and through the filter of time and nostalgia, Great Britain's wars seemed golden in success and heroics. Nelson's victory and death at Trafalgar (1805) and Wellington's defeat of Napoleon at Waterloo (1815) had acquired mythic proportions in the nation's psyche. Revenge for the death of Major-General Charles George Gordon at Omdurman in 1898 had been a glorious slaughter of the enemy. Kitchener had thrashed the Boers. What had emerged from such views of English imperialism was a cult of the personality where particular noble aristocrats achieved greatness from their wartime achievements. John Churchill won Blenheim Palace; a grateful nation raised a monument in the center of London to Lord Nelson's victory at Trafalgar; schools were named for General Gordon.

Author H. G. Wells in writing for the *Daily Chronicle* observed, "One talks and reads of the heroic age and how the world has degenerated. But indeed, this is the heroic age, suddenly come again. No legendary feats of the past, no battle with dragons or monstrous beasts, no quest or feat that man has hitherto attempted can compare with this adventure in terror, danger and splendor." Wells's collected newspaper articles later were collected as *The War That Will End War*, an idealistic phrase that President Woodrow Wilson would use only once yet would become forever associated with him.

The British upper class had been relatively unscathed by their regional wars and so viewed battle with the Central Powers as a dust-up that would end in glory. When World War I began, "'Our one great fear,' Oswald Mosley wrote, 'was that the war would be over before we got there.'" For David Mitford, another war to follow his service in the Boer War offered a heaven-sent escape from the drudgery of business. Regardless of having three children, a pregnant wife, and only one lung, he enlisted in 1915. At the time, though, Mosley and Mitford were like hundreds of other young peers who sought glory and saw their country as disintegrating under social forces that threatened to destroy the foundations of the British Empire—the foundations of their family heritage and business.

In sum, the aristocracy thought this war would readjust the proper order in England and re-establish their ordained right to lead. As historian David Cannadine summarized it,

For more than thirty years, they [the upper class] had been the object of radical (and sometimes not so radical) attack for their unjustifiable monopoly of the land, for their unearned incomes and their unearned increments, for their reactionary attitudes to social reform, for their anachronistic possession of hereditary political power, and for their leisured lifestyle and parasitic idleness... But then came the war, which gave them the supreme opportunity to prove themselves and to justify their existence. By tradition, by training, and by temperament, the aristocracy was the warrior class. They rode horses, hunted foxes, fired shot-guns. They knew how to lead, how to command, and how to look after the men in their charge.

Aristocratic institutions such as the exclusive boys' schools and universities also did their part to provide emotional and spiritual motivation. Dr. A. A. David, the headmaster of the prestigious boarding school Rugby, wrote to *The London Times*: "here is a splendid opportunity of giving a lead to young men of all classes. Here is also a supreme test of school spirit and character... To parents we would recommend a mother's advice to a hesitating son...'My boy, I don't want you to go, but if I were you, I should'" (September 2, 1914). An editorial in *The Times Educational Supplement* argued, "'Everybody recognises the fact that the spirit of discipline and sportsmanship inculcated in our schools is bearing rich and glorious fruit on the stern fields of duty, and everyone knows that many of the most stirring and heroic deeds chronicled in the war redound to the credit of young officers whose schooldays ended but a few months ago'" (September 22, 1914).

Young poet Rupert Brooke wrote:

Now, God be thanked who has matched us with his hour,
And caught our youth, and wakened us from sleeping!
With hand made sure, clear eye, and sharpened power,
To turn, as swimmers into cleanness leaping,
Glad from a world grown old and cold and weary;
Leave the sick hearts that honor could not move,
And half-men, and their dirty songs and dreary,
And all the little emptiness of love!
Oh! we, who have known shame, we have found release there,
Where there's no ill, no grief, but sleep has mending,
Naught broken save this body, lost but breath;

Nothing to shake the laughing heart's long peace there,
But only agony, and that has ending;
And the worst friend and enemy is but Death.

Young men, "wakened from sleeping," embraced this chance to prove themselves better than the "half-men" of the "old and cold and weary" century that had recently ended.

Upper-class ladies did not stint in their support of the war. Nellie Hozier, Clementine Churchill's sister, immediately went to Belgium with a nursing unit entirely financed by Lord and Lady Manners. Clementine and other ladies like her staffed canteens for soldiers or for men who worked at home in war-related industries. Other ladies offered their great houses to be used as hospitals. The list of houses was a lengthy one, including Highclere Castle, Cliveden, Attingham Park, Dunham Massey, Polesden Lacey, and many more. Few people really believed that the many medical sites would be filled to capacity with patients in a few short months.

As a measure of the gentlemanly terms on which they expected to fight in 1914, British officers took 53,000 horses to France. Colonel Douglas Haig, veteran of the Boer Wars, still believed that cavalry, lances, and sabers were quite effective. Once arrived near Menin in Belgium, English cavalry officers found "a Belgian Calvary riding school, where some exuberant young British officers put their horses over the jumps even as shells fell nearby."

Initially, class distinctions were still observed in segregated living quarters, meals, latrines, hospitals, and burial plots. Generals recruited their personal staffs from the upper class: the troops called them "Red Tabs" for the red insignia of their lapels. Aristocrats still attempted to enjoy many customary luxuries:

The Marquis of Granby ordered meat, chocolate, and pates from Fortnum & Mason twice per month. In fact, the elegant Fortnum & Mason was doing a roaring trade with well-heeled officers. From the autumn of 1914, they were able to order provisions from a special catalogue. Fortnum's offered a range of hampers. 'Parcels Post Box No. 7'...included '25 Partagas Coronas Cigars, 100 Grand Format Cigarettes, 1 F & M Plum Pudding, 1 Tin F&M Pressed Caviar, 1 Tin F & M Galantine Game (truffled), and 1 Air Cushion.' Officers could order more or less anything they wanted—from crystallized and glace fruits, tins of sardines, best Dorset butter, potted meats (various), Oxford sausages and pate de foie gras to Tunis dates, Elvas plums, and muscatels and dessert almonds.

At the battle of Sharpenburg some officers "unloaded picnic hampers from their car. Seated on a rug, they continued watching the attack while eating, and drinking claret." At least one officer had *Country Life* [magazine] sent out to the trenches as the symbol of what he was fighting for." Such genial wartime experiences were soon replaced by brutal reality. "One Grenadier officer placed an order with Fortnum & Mason for two pounds of coffee each week, though he only survived to drink a month's worth." The grandson of the Duke of Westminster wrote his mother, "'Supply me with socks and chocolates which are the two absolute necessities of life.'" Six days later he died, shot through the head.

World War I began as a conflict in which the British military expected to dominate immediately. General Kitchener "had always thought poorly of France's forces, telling Lloyd George in 1911 that, in the event of war, the Germans would 'walk through them [the French] like partridges.'" Accordingly, Britain initially sent only a small force of 84,000 men as a British Expeditionary Force (BEF) to shore up a gap between the English Channel and the French lines. At the First Battle of Ypres, Belgium (October 19-November 22,1914), 8,000 Britons were dead, 30,000 wounded, and nearly 20,000 were missing. After the brutality of the first attacks, Sir John French, who led the BEF, disparaged the French while attempting to keep his troops out of combat.

The carnage of this war has been well-documented, but even a cursory examination of the loss of life is shocking. As the war continued, military planners believed that trenches dug from Switzerland to the English Channel would provide a firm barrier against the Central Powers, never imagining how soldiers would become trapped by both trenches and disease. Any assault through the barbed wire of No Man's Land was practically suicidal: "the price of seven hundred mutilated yards in one attack was twenty-six thousand men." Soldiers suffered trench foot and other diseases in these befouled, muddy trenches never designed for extended use. On an average day, 2,500 men on both sides died. By 1915 the Germans added the insidious use of poison gas: "men drowned in it [the gas] as it dissolved their lungs." At the second Battle of Ypres on (April 22, 1915), "five thousand French soldiers died within ten minutes." In the Battle of the Somme (July-November 1916), over a million people died. In 1917 alone, 800,000 British soldiers were killed or injured.

Only the severely wounded British soldiers were evacuated back home to "Old Blighty" (the British Isles). Those with minor injuries were treated and returned to battle to go "over the top" of the trenches again as soon as possible.

The war had begun with battles on horseback; by 1917 armored tanks wreaked carnage and destruction to a degree that had never been possible with horse-borne soldiers. Men not only suffered physical injuries but were also left shell-shocked – post-traumatic stress syndrome in today's kinder military understanding. Any men who fled were tried as deserters and quickly shot. The once-cheery song, "It's A Long Way to Tipperary," now seemed merely mournful.

The upper class was not unique in the loss of life, but the fact of loss at all was initially unfathomable to the class. In the first three months of the war, the exclusive boys' schools which had zealously encouraged enlistment counted great losses: "Eton had lost sixty-five of its former pupils; Wellington thirty-eight; Charterhouse and Harrow, twenty-one each; Rugby, twenty." Thirty-one percent of the Oxford University Class of 1913 were killed. By the end of that first year, "the death toll included six peers, sixteen baronets, ninety-five sons of peers, and eighty-two sons of baronets." World War I was especially deadly for aristocrats because "officers were far more likely to be killed than the men whom they led over the parapets of trenches and into machine-gun fire" precisely because they became the first and strategically-significant targets. At the First Battle of Ypres (Belgium; 19 October-22 November 1914), the British Expeditionary Force lost most of their entire force to wounds or death; the casualty rate for officers was nearly 97 per cent. Roughly 12 percent of all British soldiers who took part in the war were killed, but for peers or sons of peers in uniform the figure was 19 percent. By 1917 a fifth of aristocrats who were then serving in the war died because of war wounds. Prime Ministers Herbert Asquith and Andrew Bonar Law both lost sons.

The initial impulse of the public was to resist the news of slaughter. Disbelieving Britons embraced as true a short story, "The Bowmen," published in the *London Evening News* (September 1914) by Welsh writer Arthur Machen. The brief story recounts that British fighters in the Battle of Mons knew that they were outnumbered and yet fought with a jaunty, undeterred spirit:

> All morning the German guns had thundered and shrieked against this
> corner, and against the thousand or so of men who held it. The men joked

at the shells, and found funny names for them, and had bets about them, and greeted them with scraps of music-hall songs. But the shells came on and burst, and tore good Englishmen limb from limb, and tore brother from brother, and as the heat of the day increased so did the fury of that terrific cannonade. There was no help, it seemed." Finally, one of the British soldiers recalled the Latin motto... *"Adsit Anglis Sanctus Georgius"* – "May St. George be a present help to the English." The soldier cried out this motto and—like the myth of the once and future King Arthur—hundreds of ghostly bowmen who once fought at the Battle of Agincourt came to their rescue: They were like men who drew the bow, and with another shout, their cloud of arrows flew singing and tingling through the air towards the German hosts.

The fantasy concluded by announcing that ten thousand Germans were killed and that the English army held their ground. Anxious readers clung to the notion that heavenly force was on the British side rather than believe the initial brutal reports of the war in Flanders' fields.

A true story emerged from the early months that seemed to promise that the war could, perhaps, stay more gentlemanly than it appeared. Up and down the Western Front on Christmas Eve 1914, Germans and English began singing "Silent Night." One German set up a Christmas tree for both sides to see. Cautiously they called out to each other across No Man's Land and communicated that they would like a truce. They collected their dead, exchanged sausages for chocolate, shared drinks, even played football (soccer) together during the twenty-four hours of peace. By Christmas afternoon, "thousands of British and German soldiers were trading cigarettes, helmets, canned food, and other souvenirs, taking pictures, and singing carols in both languages."

There were also attempts to humanize the support of the troops. One royal effort consisted of sending "Every British soldier. . . an embossed brass box of cigarettes, pipe, and tobacco (or another gift for nonsmokers, such as spices for Indian troops) and a Christmas card from the royal couple, showing the Queen in broad choker necklace and crown and the King in his field marshal's uniform." Eventually such gestures collapsed under the weight of the ongoing conflict.

Soldiers who wrote home tried to shield their loved ones from the horrors they faced. Family members on the home front, however, came to see the highly efficient telegraph carriers as messengers of death and averted their eyes, praying and willing them to bicycle past. As the mounting death rates rose among the upper class, some of the aristocrats began to oppose the war or attempt to have their sons avoid physical danger. Lord Lansdowne – former viceroy of India, secretary for war, and foreign secretary – had initially supported the war; however, early in the fighting he had lost a son. After the Battle of the Somme in 1916, he began to doubt the need to battle to an unconditional victory. He was particularly appalled by the number of British officers slain: "'We are slowly but surely killing off the best of the male population of these islands…,' he had written to Asquith, then prime minister. 'Generations will have to come and go before the country recovers from the loss.'" Rudyard Kipling, who also lost a son in the war, called Lansdowne a coward and an "old imbecile." Eventually, "Lansdownism" became a term describing a distrust of those in the upper class who were "defeatists" and not fully supportive of the war.

Some among the upper class took advantage of their social and political connections in order to save their sons. The Duchess of Rutland was able to have her son, the Marquis of Granby, medically discharged from battlefield service in 1915 even though his entry medical report had shown him to be fit. At the very same time his father, the Duke of Rutland, was raising thousands of men from his estates and nearby villages to serve in the North Midlanders by charging them that "The more of you who go, the quicker the war will be over. Come Forward. This is what I want. And what England wants. And I am confident that what England wants, you will not forget to give her."

The country did indeed want its men to enlist. The Royal Flying Corps (forerunner of the Royal Air Force) was only two years old at the start of the war. Production of their most famous fighter plane, the Sopwith Camel, did not begin until the war was two years advanced. The combination of inexperienced pilots and unreliable aircraft technology meant that a pilot had a life expectancy of two weeks. Pilots were desperately needed, but most knew that their enlistment was a death sentence. At the beginning of the conflict the War Office established the army standard that a man had to be five foot eight to be enlisted; after two months of horrifically deadly losses, the requirement had dropped to five foot three. By mid-war, the extraordinary practice of mandatory conscription became necessary. The Conscription Act did permit exemptions for conscientious objectors such as Quakers, but in "practice 'conchies' were treated as criminals." An unprecedented practice of shaming men to enlist encouraged women to "do their bit" by giving well-bodied men white feathers, calling them out as cowards.

By November 1918, Kaiser Wilhelm could see that the huge influx of American materiel and troops had irrevocably tipped the scales against his nation. He abdicated on November 9. The guns stopped and the Armistice began at the eleventh hour on the eleventh day of the eleventh month. The physical suffering and emotional trauma would continue for decades. As for the social fabric of Britain, the loss of life among the upper class opened a social and governmental space to be filled by other classes and other value systems that had to discover ways of dealing with the wounded and the shell-shocked, the widows and orphans, and the economic and social systems that were irrevocably changed.

The statistics of death and maiming associated with World War I surpassed those of all previous wars. The total number of combatants who had died in the most recent conflict, the Boer Wars, had amounted to 60,000 dead – 22,000 of whom had been British. The conservative tabulation of World War I deaths placed the number of military deaths at 8.5 million; and an additional 12 to 13 million civilian deaths occurred through bombing, disease, torpedoed ships and other methods. Britain's portion of this carnage was extraordinarily high given its population. Nearly a million military deaths occurred; 800,000 of whom came from the tiny island itself. In fact, "…Britain…suffered more casualties in World War I than in World War II." The toll was particularly appalling among the young. Of every 20 British men between ages 18 and 32 at the outbreak of war, three were dead and six wounded when it ended. The statistics for casualty survivors were depressing as well. In Britain, 41,000 survivors had limb amputations; 10,000 were blinded; and 65,000 were treated for shell-shock, though many more were probably undiagnosed: "The human frame couldn't withstand the impact of this new, fully mechanised slaughter on a grand scale…"

The devastation of death abroad was echoed by economic privation at home. The government had gone nearly bankrupt and was forced to borrow millions of pounds sterling to finance the war. These economic stresses, though not as grievous as the deaths, would, however, be depressing, long-lasting and culture-changing for Britain.

Not surprisingly, the Armistice talks at the Paris Peace Conference (12 July 1919-20 January 1920; signed 28 June 1920) were not really negotiations. The Treaty of Versailles was bitter, punitive, and financially weighted. Ultimately, the five treaties that ended World War I "imposed on the Central Powers, especially Germany, various territorial losses, financial reparations and military restrictions. These terms were severe enough to cause lasting resentment among the defeated, particularly in Germany, which was hit hardest and also had to accept a war guilt clause that made it alone wholly responsible for the outbreak of World War I." Even the United States Congress refused to ratify the Treaty of Versailles. Regardless of whatever revenge it may have savored with the treaty, the war's aftermath would leave Britain a country reeling from the war and unaware that it had deeply planted the seeds of yet another world war.

CHAPTER 10

NO MORE "ENJOYABLE WARS": DAVID MITFORD AND WINSTON CHURCHILL IN THE GREAT WAR

Bertie Mitford's second son, David, had escaped from his dreary office job at the *Lady* and to the battlefield for only a few months before the cold and rain of the Western Front had taken a toll on his remaining lung. He was invalided home in January 1915. Against the wishes of his family, he returned to the front by the second Battle of Ypres in April of that year and served valiantly for two more years. By 1917, though, his health was so impaired that he was again invalided home; his war had finally ended.

David's older brother Clement had also enlisted in 1914 and was, as ever, perfection in whatever he did, soon earning the Distinguished Service Order. Like David, Clement left behind a young family, his wife Helen Olgivy Mitford – first cousin of Clementine Hozier Churchill – and a daughter, Rosemary. Helen was pregnant with their second child, whom they hoped would be a son and the Mitford heir.

Shortly after David returned to Europe, Clement's battalion was moved eastward into Belgium. The Mitford sons could now count among their comrade-in-arms on the continent John Kipling, the only son of war hawk Rudyard Kipling. John had been rejected by the Royal Navy and the army due to his severe short-sightedness, but Rudyard had pulled every social tie he had to secure a commission for his son. John was killed in 1915 just six weeks after his eighteenth birthday, his body lost amid the carnage.

Thirty-eight-year-old Clement Mitford died the same year at Walloon Brabant, Belgium. His death was devastating to the aging Bertie, who idolized his eldest son. Clement's death also placed the grief-stricken Helen in the precarious position of holding the fate of her family within her body: if she bore a son, he would inherit the title and estates; if she bore a girl, all would go to her brother-in-law David.

Clement and Helen Mitford's second child would be named Clementine.

As such, when Algernon Bertram Freeman-Mitford, 1st Baron Redesdale, passed away in 1916, by the rule of primogeniture his second son David unexpectedly and sadly acquired the title of 2nd Baron Redesdale. With the title came an estate that, if managed carefully, would permanently free David from the job he hated and support a family that would swell in size to seven children.

This single family was a microcosm of the disorientation experienced by the English upper class in the twentieth century. No movie wants greater drama than that presented by the love stories, affairs, tragic deaths, treacherous politics, beauty, brilliance, war and extravagance of the Mitford children. The eldest, Nancy, drew the family into national notoriety and celebrity with semi-autobiographical fiction novels that told family secrets and conflicts, even about her love affair with a French architect of the Peace of Versailles. Pamela was one of a string of six women married to a brilliant physicist vital to the Royal Air Force during World War II. Tom requested to fight in Burma rather than invade the Germany he had loved. Diana married a Guinness heir; then left him and their two sons for a fascist politician. Once considered the most beautiful woman in England, she became the most hated. Unity Mitford so passionately adored Adolf Hitler that she stalked him in restaurants. Jessica eloped with a cousin to get to the Spanish Civil War. Finally, youngest sibling Deborah would marry Andrew Cavendish and eventually become chatelaine of one of the greatest estates in England.

**

For his part, in 1914 Winston Churchill was ebullient at the prospect of war with Germany, though he would later ruefully reflect that it was not, like the

Boer War, an "enjoyable war." He had been President of the Board of Trade and the Home Secretary, but he wanted to be in the cabinet as his father had been before him. Germany's military buildup first and directly challenged the Royal Navy, so it was there he wanted to be assigned. Despite his lack of naval experience, he lobbied to be First Lord of the Admiralty. Prime Minister Asquith offered the position, and he ecstatically accepted.

Churchill threw himself into the job with a passion. He quickly had the navy move to Scapa Flow in Scotland from which vantage point they could safely monitor the German naval activity. He lobbied for full mobilization of the navy and went ahead with those plans without cabinet approval – a consent which they grudgingly gave after the fact. However, when the war finally arrived, no one could dispute Churchill's brilliant foresight in having British warships prepared to instantly blockade the German navy in their ports. He was not infallible in his insights. On September 21, 1914, he affirmed that the Germans were now afraid to leave their ports, and the next day three British ships were torpedoed and sunk. Still, he was not content with just supervision of the navy. He seemed willing to manage all areas of government without invitation, suggesting that Britain give China to the Japanese in order to gain the Japanese as allies, that the Irish were disloyal in seeking Home Rule with war at hand, that his marines should attack at Antwerp even though they lacked ammunition and training. He advised the army on how to direct their combatants, and he made regular trips to France to survey the troops. In a stunning show of confidence, he finally asked Prime Minister Asquith to give him a military rank and allow him to take over the running of the war. This aggressive enthusiasm gave Churchill firm admirers and fierce detractors.

Despite Churchill's zeal in preparing the Navy for war, he made significant miscalculations in judgment concerning the conduct of the war. In February 1915 Churchill boldly offered a strategy that he claimed would save The Triple Entente (Britain, France, Russia) from the slaughter mounting in the trenches of Europe: he proposed to open a second front on the Black Sea. If his navy could control the Dardanelles – the waters between the Mediterranean and Black Seas – the allies would isolate the Ottoman Empire, link themselves to their ally Russia, stress the resources of the enemy, and force defections from the Central Powers.

The plan went awry almost from the start. General Kitchener, who had never liked the uppity Churchill, stated he could not spare troops. Sea

Lord Fisher vacillated in his commitment to and assessment of the plan. Intelligence and maps were inaccurate. Churchill confidently persuaded the War Cabinet that the Navy could succeed on its own if the army could not spare troops. The Navy alone was not enough, and though troops were urgently requested, five weeks elapsed before they arrived. In the meantime, the enemy was able to prepare their resistance, German submarines arrived to attack the battleships, and the Navy had to withdraw, leaving the troops without naval artillery support. These miscalculations guaranteed the slaughter of 45,000 Allies at the Gallipoli peninsula and nearly a quarter of a million Allied casualties overall.

Reports said the green waters of the Aegean turned red with the blood.

Both the public and politicians were horrified and outraged. Although there was a wealth of blame to share for the fiasco, Churchill's brash intervention, his very public bragging, and his independent handling of the Navy made him appear more a freebooter than a thoughtful naval leader. Opposition leader Bonar Law called for his dismissal from office. Even leaders within his party were relieved when he tendered his resignation as Lord of the Admiralty on November 15, 1915.

Undeterred, Winston then immediately requested a military rank and assignment. Four days after his resignation, Major Winston Churchill left with his servant for France to join the Oxfordshire Yeomanry, leaving Clementine instructions to send three bottles of brandy every fortnight. The limitation of being a major immediately chafed him. Within seven months he secured release from the army and returned to London to badger the Prime Minister for some larger role in the war. An official inquiry into the debacle of the Dardanelles had eventually concluded that Churchill should not bear entire blame: Prime Minister Asquith, it was said, had not kept Churchill informed; General Kitchener, it was said, had caused ruinous delays. Accordingly, Lloyd George found enough political cover to allow himself in July 1917 to appoint Churchill to the position of Ministry of Munitions, a position he held until the end of the war with a relative absence of controversy and with an eerie prescience of mind to urge the development of tank technology that proved vital in the next war.

November 1922 brought another type of stress to the family: for the first time in over two decades, Churchill was out of office: "'In the twinkling of an eye I found myself without an office, without a sea, without a party, and even without an appendix.'"

Yet for decades Churchill would wander in a political desert, his enemies taunting him with the phrase, "Remember the Dardanelles." It is quite possible that Prime Minister Winston Churchill during World War II delayed the direct-front amphibious assault of D-Day because he feared another Dardanelles.

CHAPTER 11

THE WASTELAND OF MEMORY AND REACTION

They shall grow not old, as we that are left grow old:
Age shall not weary them, nor the years condemn.
At the going down of the sun and in the morning,
We will remember them.

Robert Laurence Binyon, For The Fallen (September 1914)

April is the cruellest month, breeding
Lilacs out of the dead land, mixing
Memory and desire...

T. S. Eliot, The Wasteland (1922)

A few weeks after the Armistice that ended The Great War, tiny carrot-topped Marigold was born to Winston and Clementine Churchill. The Churchills had pet names for all of their children: 12-year old Diana was "the gold-cream kitten"; 10-year old Randolph, "the Rabbit"; and 7-year old Sarah, "the Bumblebee." To her parents, the birth of this new baby, whom they called "Duckadilly," seemed a welcome sign that they had finally made it through the war and that life could resume its way again. Thirty-three months later, Marigold contracted an illness that progressed into septicemia. Her blood pressure dropped precipitously, making her feverish and causing painfully labored breathing. Clementine watched in horror as her daughter's condition deteriorated: one day Marigold asked her mother to sing her favorite song, "I'm Forever Blowing Bubbles," and Clementine could not even whisper the words. On August 19, 1921, Winston and Clementine were at the side of their Duckadilly as she died. Winston grieved that this little life had "'been extinguished just when it was so beautiful & so happy – just when it was beginning.'" Clementine was inconsolable. She shrieked and cried "'like an animal in mortal pain.'" A last child, Mary, was born the following year, and they lavished their love upon her; but Duckadilly's death stayed with them. For the rest of her life, Clementine would never be able to speak of Marigold.

The year 1921 had already proved an *annus horribilis* for the Churchill family. On April 14 while in Paris, Clementine's 33-year-old brother, Lt. Commander William Ogilvy Hozier of the Royal Navy, shot and killed himself. In June, Churchill's mother—the indomitable Jennie Jerome Churchill – died from an accident that had initially seemed minor. On a smaller, personal scale, these deaths evoked the emotional breakdown of the country of Britain after The Great War. Britons were left disoriented by grief over the incomprehensible loss of life, the psychological and physical trauma for survivors of the battlefield; and they felt an intense need to assign blame and punishment upon Germany for the carnage and financial devastation wreaked upon Britain.

The national wartime unity had disappeared with unnerving speed. Agitation resumed in Britain among women and other workers for the vote, better jobs, and increased pay. Some people chose a grief-stricken retreat into memories and a reactionary impulse to return to a romanticized pre-war life. Others, convinced that traditional values in art, personal relationships, and politics had led the country to this horrific disaster, angrily rejected all conventions as broken. All felt bewildered and untethered from the traditions that had once seemed good and dependable. Gertrude Stein would call this a "lost generation" wandering in what T. S. Eliot named the "waste land" of modern life. Aristocrats saw in it a crumbling of the Empire itself.

The apotheosis and remembrances of the World War I dead were extensive, heart-rending affirmations avowing that the sacrifices of these slain Britons were not in vain and would not be forgotten. In 1915 after the Second Battle of Ypres, Canadian physician John McCrae wrote the poem "In Flanders Fields" for the funeral of a friend. This now-famous rondeau chronicles the voices of the war dead whispering to the war's survivors. McCrae begins by juxtaposing images of life and death, poppies standing against the cold cemetery markers and the songs of larks drowned by gunfire:

> In Flanders fields the poppies blow
> Between the crosses, row on row,
> That mark our place; and in the sky
> The larks, still bravely singing, fly
> Scarce heard amid the guns below.

The speakers wistfully mourn the fragile lives they so recently, so easily, left:

> We are the Dead. Short days ago
> We lived, felt dawn, saw sunset glow,
> Love and were loved, and now we lie
> In Flanders fields.

> Finally, they warn that they must never be forgotten:
> Take up our quarrel with the foe:
> To you from failing hands we throw
> The torch; be yours to hold it high.
> If ye break faith with us who die
> We shall not sleep, though poppies grow
> In Flanders fields.

Their survivors must continue the fight or else forever be haunted for breaking faith with those who gave their lives.

The power of this guilt-charged sentiment was potent at the time and has persisted to the present day. On the centenary of the start of World War I, the British affirmed their faithful remembrance with an art display of ceramic poppies cascading like bleeding tears down the Tower of London.

The 2014 London commemorations had much in common with memorials that arose in postwar years throughout the battlegrounds of Europe and in Britain itself. In Ypres, Belgium, a bas relief memorial shows a dead British soldier flanked by women mourning his death, the British lion roaring its grief. Ascending heavenward like Christ, this soldier is accompanied by an angel carrying a sword and a laurel crown, signaling immortality and reward for his bravery in battle. At the Menin Gate in this same town and for a hundred years, every evening a poem of remembrance is read, a mournful trumpet sounds its salute, and flowers are laid to give thanks for the sacrifice of the fallen soldiers. The nearby Tyne Cot cemetery holds carefully tended graves planted with flowers. These remembrances of the war dead provided comfort by affirming and memorializing the rightness of their cause.

A practical aspect of some of the more elaborate memorials was that they offered the only focal point possible when the fallen were never recovered or never properly identified. In the heat of battle, army chaplains could only write a soldier's name on a slip of paper, slip it into a bottle at the burial site, and hope the location might later be marked by a wooden cross. The British government undertook to establish an Imperial War Graves Commission (IWGC) to take whatever action necessary to insure a respectful grave or remembrance for each soldier from the British Commonwealth. Rudyard Kipling, shaken by his son John's death at the Battle of Loos, gave time and money to the IWGC, writing special inscriptions and donating his own specially-designed memorials to the cemeteries.

At home, the British government commissioned famous architect Edwin Lutyens to design an empty tomb as a poignant reminder of the soldiers who would never return to their homeland. On November 11, 1920, when King George V unveiled this Cenotaph in the middle of Whitehall – one of the busiest streets in London – " he tossed "a handful of the soil from a Flanders battlefield into the grave." A paired commemoration was the entombing of Britain's Unknown Warrior in Westminster Abbey. During the ceremony the entire nation was silent and it was reported that no noise could be heard except for the sound of sobbing women. For decades, buses would literally stop in London on November 11 at the eleventh hour and stand quiet for two minutes in remembrance.

This war haunted England.

A different form of remembrance began to take the form of seething rage. Literary works like Eric Remarque's *All Quiet on the Western Front*, Robert Graves's *Goodbye to All That*, and poetry by Wilfred Owen and Siegfried Sassoon fed a simmering conviction that the entire war had been pointless. The poem "Dulce et Decorum Est" (published posthumously in 1920) was penned by Wilfred Owen, who died one week before the end of the war. His graphic imagery confronted readers with the brutality of modern trench warfare and the new military demon of poison gas:

If in some smothering dreams you too could pace
Behind the wagon that we flung him in,
And watch the white eyes writhing in his face,
His hanging face, like a devil's sick of sin;
If you could hear, at every jolt, the blood
Come gargling from the froth-corrupted lungs,
Obscene as cancer, bitter as the cud
Of vile, incurable sores on innocent tongues, -
My friend, you would not tell with such high zest
To children ardent for some desperate glory,
The old Lie: *Dulce et Decorum est/*
Pro patria mori.
(It is sweet and right for one to die for one's country).

It was not sweet and right to die, argued the disillusioned. In their view, young people, betrayed by the flawed values and military strategies of an older generation, had faced needless slaughter.

Persuaded that civilization itself had been at fault, the upstart Modernist movement rejected traditional values in art and politics. Political protests against traditional laws became violent. Suffragettes attempted to bomb Parliament, invaded the House of Commons. and made physical assaults upon Winston Churchill and other members of Parliament. With uneasy eyes some Britons wondered whether the very monarchy would be overthrown, as had happened in Russia in 1917.

The traditional grounding of the English economy was broken as well. A Spanish flu pandemic killed hundreds and reduced the workforce. Miners called a general strike in 1926 to agitate for better pay and working conditions. Traditional jobs vanished altogether, all because of wartime exigencies. For the first time in human history, the mass-production of clothes had been necessitated because of the millions of soldiers needing uniforms. This single fact reconfigured the clothing industry, developing new ways of distributing goods—such as through department stores—and so shifting emphasis onto an urban economy. Economic power shifted from the land – the foundation of the upper class – to urban centers governed by captains of industry and populated with workers untethered from the land.

Even at a social level, upper-class society struggled with the codes, privacy, and discretion that had been bulwarks of their class. Clementine Churchill's sister Nellie went against family opinion to marry Bertram Romilly, a Lieutenant-Colonel in the Scots Guard, and went to live with him in Galilee and Egypt. With a similar disregard for social opinion, their son Esmond would elope with David Mitford's daughter who would join him to fight with the Republicans and Communists in the Spanish Civil War.

In a further shock to the Churchills—and to social England – Duchess Consuelo Vanderbilt Churchill divorced her husband, the 9th Duke of Marlborough in 1921. The divorce was sensational and its aftermath bizarre. The Duke married his paramour Gladys Deacon, who became increasingly eccentric and was said to dine with a revolver by the side of her plate. Eventually she and the Duke came to such odds that he turned off the water, heat, and power at Blenheim in order to drive her out. This public exposure of the misadventures of the elite class amounted to a social weapon that could be used against them. Writer P. G. Wodehouse's stories about a butler Jeeves who was far wiser than his aristocratic employer reinforced a perception about the upper class as being foolish and unworthy of the wealth they possessed.

Further, the government itself seemed bent upon stripping the upper class of its inherited land and wealth. The war had virtually bankrupted Britain, and, on top of that, the United States expected repayment of a $333 billion debt – with interest. Beyond this debt, Britain needed medical care and pensions for veterans and to build homes that Lloyd George said should be "worthy of heroes" or for their widows and orphans. Although the Budget of 1909 had insured that the upper class were paying taxes, the financial consequences of The Great War forced even higher rates of taxation upon the only people who had any financial reserves available to be taxed. By 1919 lords such as the Earl of Carnarvon experienced increased income tax rates of 60%.

A monumental problem faced by peers of the realm was that they had more assets in land and art than in the more liquid asset of cash investments. Faced with houses they could no longer staff and taxes that they must pay, they turned to all methods they could imagine in order to acquire revenue. Some landowners rushed hundreds of acres of land into sale, which further depressed land values. Some rented out their houses, furnished. Others sold artwork that had been acquired over the centuries. The Castle Howard estate sold over 110 Old Masters and a thousand rare books. At Blenheim the Duke of Marlborough sold eighteen Rubens and over a dozen Van Dycks. Debt had now become a significant legacy of one generation to the next. To pay his father's death duties and his father's business debts, the 10th Duke of Devonshire

Edward Cavendish watched his 24 books printed by William Caxton and 1,347 volumes of plays – including four Shakespeare folios and 39 Shakespeare quartos—cross the Atlantic to the Huntington Library in California. He then sold tens of thousands of acres of land in Somerset, Sussex, and Derbyshire; the family's London mansion Devonshire House; and, in 1929, the elegant Palladian villa in west London, Chiswick House. The great glass conservatory at Chatsworth, which had required ten men and quantities of coal to run it, was simply demolished as an economy measure. Finally, Devonshire House itself – so famous for its 1897 party – was demolished and its gates sold to sit at an entrance to the Green Park in London.

Into this setting came aggressive American collectors to find the bargains. George Washington Vanderbilt, Andrew Mellon, Henry Clay Frick, J. P. Morgan, and William Randolph Hearst made huge acquisitions of treasures: "Henry Clay Folger bought every Shakespeare First Folio he could lay hands on…" and carried them back to Washington, D. C. to establish his Folger Library Gallery. Others, like William Randolph Hearst who purchased St. Donat's, bought great houses, castles, entire estates. In 1925 Thomas C. Williams purchased Agecroft Hall, "a handsome Tudor manor in Lancashire, which was taken to pieces, packed into numbered crates, and shipped to Richmond, Virginia, where it was reassembled and still proudly stands." Convinced that their architectural history was being destroyed by the new fashion for modern conveniences and designs, angered by the American plunderers, convinced that a desirable way of life was passing away, the aristocracy became entrenched.

Those peers who did retain wealth sought to resist change by maintaining the standards and practices of their golden era. Before the Great War, Lady Carnarvon had given a great dinner party in the Karnak Temple in Egypt with staff from the Winter Palace Hotel dressed in costumes inspired by the *A Thousand and One Nights*. Then, as though unfazed by the war, in 1920 Lady Carnarvon invited hundreds of guests to a fabulous debutante ball for her daughter that ended only with the dawn. Two years later she gave an engagement ball for her son to which she invited 1,000 people. This was all at a time when Lord Carnarvon was questing for the tomb of Tutankhamen. He found the tomb in 1922 but at a withering cost of £50,000 pounds ($4 million in 2019 value).

Some young nobles wanted to put the survivors' guilt and darkness behind them and use any family wealth to live a high life. The interwar years—the Roaring Twenties of the United States—in England was called "the era of the

Bright Young Things, gossip columns, night clubs, cocktails, shorter skirts, and dancing."

Coming out balls still continued for debutantes such as Nancy Mitford (1923), Pamela Mitford (1924), Diane Mitford (1928), Diana Churchill (1928), Unity Mitford (1932), Sarah Churchill (1933), Jessica Mitford (1935), and Deborah Mitford (1938). Diana Manners, the "Helen" to whom Winston Churchill had allotted a thousand ships, remained so immensely beautiful and charismatic that Cynthia Asquith wrote that when she left a room "'brightness fell from the air.'" Her marriage to Duff Cooper in 1919 was one of the Season's premier social events.

The Old Guard seemed to retreat to their country estates, and the new social swirl now included an American syndicate of people such as Nancy Astor and Emerald Cunard. By 1936 when Wallis Simpson made herself the romantic obsession of the heir to the throne, this particular American "buccaneer" proved to be the last straw for traditionalists. Edward VIII was forced to choose between the Crown and Mrs. Simpson, a decision for which Winston Churchill tried to gain time. In some quarters, the dilemma was a romantic one. However, for many Britons, who longed for stability in their lives and government, the choice seemed clear: Edward could maintain the meaning of the Crown and the traditions of England – or discard the heritage of English values for a twice-divorced American. The country was appalled and sent reeling when Edward decided to abdicate. The center, indeed, did not seem to hold.

A growing political response to this disorienting upheaval of standards and traditions and the destabilizing possibilities of Socialism was to seek safety in an authoritarian system: Fascism. This movement especially gained force in the 1920s in Italy and in Germany who resented the punishments inflicted upon them by the victors of World War I and sought strong leaders to regain the power and honor of their nations. The movement also became attractive in Britain. The aristocracy in particular could see that a firm hand was needed to right a ship of state that was clearly off course. The Spanish Civil War of 1936-39, in that sense, was a test between Socialism and Fascism in which Franco's fascists prevailed. Germany, which had supported the fascist leader Franco saw its opportunity to gradually breach the Versailles Treaty and remilitarize the Rhineland. Frankly, there was large popular sentiment that the settlement terms of World War I had been unconscionably punitive. Later Hitler would continue this pattern of incremental redress for World War I punishments until he finally broke new ground and launched his campaign for political domination. He encouraged his country by promising to regain its honor and greatness in the world.

***

Amid a wrenching realignment of post-war politics and culture, David Mitford's children came to maturity: Nancy (b.1904), Pamela (b. 1907), Thomas (b. 1909), Diana (b. 1910), Unity (b. 1914), Jessica (b. 1917), and Deborah (b. 1920). Brother Clement's death during the war had been the price for allowing David to escape employment, and David—like many of his countrymen— dutifully memorialized his soldier-brother with pews contributed to the Swinbrook. Once he assumed the title and lands as Baron, David—like many of his peers – hoped that England would return to its pre-war ways and that he could float on the current of his inherited wealth. However, Bertie Mitford had invested so much money in the country house Batsford that the family needed to sell it in 1919 to pay taxes and still have a comfortable annual income. As a result, the Mitfords had a title, were socially well-connected, and had a degree of wealth that was grand by middle-class standards but modest by upper-class standards of ducal families such as the Marlboroughs. The Mitfords were firmly established on the fringes of the highest aristocratic circle.

Familial connections among the elite remained important forms of social currency. Even a cursory examination of the relationships among the Mitfords and Churchills suggests the numerous, complex ties within the class. Bertie Mitford's reputed lover was the mother of Clementine Hozier Churchill, and so David Mitford may have been Clementine's half-brother rather than just her cousin. Bertie Mitford's eldest son Clement married Helen Hozier, a cousin of Clementine Hozier Churchill. Clementine's nephew Esmond Romilly would marry Bertie Mitford's granddaughter, Jessica Mitford. The Churchills' eldest daughter Diana was a flower girl at Diana Mitford's wedding to Bryan Guinness. Diana Mitford often enjoyed extended visits and house parties at Clementine and Winston Churchill's country house, Chartwell. The Churchill's son Randolph had a teenage crush on her. Randolph also relentlessly criticized his cousin Unity Mitford for her crush on Hitler. Such connections of class and family would be severely tested in World War II.

CHAPTER 12

THE MITFORD CHILDREN BETWEEN THE WARS

Why did I dedicate the beastly book [*Highland Fling*] at all, as I said to Muv *other* people can dedicate books without this sort of thing happening but she & Farve appear to think I did it to annoy them. Then they say that as I'm nearly thirty I ought to stop going out at all. Why? And what should I do if I did stop. I can't make out what they really want me to do. Live permanently in the country I suppose.

Oh dear I do feel miserable.

(Nancy Mitford in a letter to her sister Diana, March 1931)

The problem with Nancy Mitford's publication of *Highland Fling* was not its dedication to her supposed fiancé so much as the fact that this first novel was clearly a mocking, thinly-disguised description of her family and friends. "Muv" (Nancy's mother Sydney) and "Farve" (her father David) were apoplectic at multiple levels: Nancy's engagement to Hamish St. Clair-Erskine was not official and might not even be real; all of their social group would recognize the characters and be offended; most humiliatingly, the flippant novel was a blindsiding public assault upon themselves. The cheeriest familial response came from Nancy's Uncle George who gingerly suggested that the book was "awfully indecent but ... [I hope] it will sell."

This moment of controversy typified Nancy's career of witty, semi-autobiographical writing, acerbic challenges to the traditional values and expectations of her parents' generation. Several of her siblings would later write their versions of the remarkable, charged Mitford childhoods; however, it was Nancy, the eldest, who first discovered the market for semi-autobiographical stories about the country life adventures of a quirky family of genteel poverty. Nancy's writing propelled her family into a notoriety that would deservedly surround all of them for the rest of their lives.

***

Nancy Freeman-Mitford, born November 28, 1904, was aged twelve when her father inherited his title and she acquired the prefix "Honourable." She believed in class-consciousness – especially in the intellectual and social superiority of herself and of her friends—and always regarded herself as a person who deserved the advantages and leisure of aristocrats. Her 1954 essay "The English Aristocracy" (*Encounter* magazine, ed. Stephen Spender; 1954) was tongue-in-cheek; but its judgments of the differences between the Upper Class and everyone else – between "U" and "non-U" (Us and not-Us) – was satire based upon her class-consciousness.

As a child Nancy felt her parents deprived her of the social life and educational advantages of her class by rearing her away from urban excitement in a small country house and taught by governesses whom she deemed stupid. She turned to sharpening her wit by tormenting her younger sisters. She mocked Pamela for being sickly and claimed that Diana's head was unnaturally large. When Jessica and Deborah were playing in the churchyard and fell into a newly-dug grave, she told them "it meant 'bad luck,' forever." She nicknamed her youngest sister "Nine," saying it was her mental age and calling her by that name until Deborah married. It was with relief that at age sixteen she was freed of governesses and attended the Hatherop Castle School.

In contradiction to her jaundiced view of her parents, David and Sydney financed Nancy's travels with four girlfriends to Italy and France, and in 1923 funded her debutante year though she defied them by "bobbing" her hair and slipping out of parent-supervised balls to visit night clubs. She announced she was unofficially engaged to Hamish St Clair-Erskine, an unadmitted homosexual who was rumored to have had a sexual fling with her brother Tom while at Eton. The most life-changing result of her social debut, though, was that she instantly became popular with the smart set of post-war England: The Bright Young Things (BYT). With what Brian Howard called her "pyrotechnical" wit, she settled in with a sybaritic Oxford group who shared her sardonic humor: Howard, the model for Anthony Blanche in *Brideshead Revisited*, author Evelyn Waugh, photographer Cecil Beaton, and poet John Betjeman. Her father found these friends intolerable, one time shouting to Sydney in front of them, "'Have these people no homes of their own?'" These rising literary and artistic lights would be Nancy's lifelong friends.

To gain financial independence from her parents and to finance her social life, Nancy began a guest column in her grandfather's magazine, *The Lady*, entitled *"The Shooting Party, Some Hints for the Woman Guest* by the Hon. Nancy Mitford." Her witty column whetted people's interest for gossip about upper class social life and soon lead to publication in *Vogue* and *Harper's Bazaar*.

It was her novels, though, that brought her the money and fame she desired. Through them she entertained her friends – and, importantly, a paying audience – by revealing some of the luxuries and foibles of her social class. Her books parodied the upper-class fetish for nicknames, a habit true in her family: Naunce (Nancy), Woman (Pamela), Tuddemy (Tom), Honks (Diana), Bobo (Unity), Decca (Jessica), Debo (Deborah), Farve (their father), and Muv (their mother). Nancy also had fertile ground from which to harvest action for her novels, writing of ineffective nannies and governesses upon whom children played merciless pranks. One governess to the Mitfords, she avowed, was best at teaching the children how to shoplift. Her parents clearly had idiosyncrasies ripe for literary harvesting: they allowed young Unity to eat "nothing but mashed potatoes for two years" because they would not force their children to eat objectionable foods. Their father David required that their bedroom windows had to be open six inches, regardless of the season or weather; he bought a miniature pony and brought him home in a cab; he invented a game in which the children lay a trail across hill and dale for the hounds to practice their tracking skills. When collecting the offering at church, he would stop twice at his sister's pew and nudge her until she slapped "his hand, which started us on the peculiar agony of church giggles." Perhaps unsurprisingly in 1938 he purchased a small Scottish island, Inch Kenneth, as a personal getaway for himself.

In her fiction and memoirs Nancy caricatured Farve into a harsher, less whimsical man and Muv into a woman who seemed detached from her children and from all practical matters. Farve/Uncle Matthew and his friends on horseback were presented as literally hunting the children as substitutes for a fox. In a memoir Nancy recorded an incident in which Unity told Sydney that Jessica is going to kill herself, and their mother continues what she is doing with the comment, "'I hope she won't do anything so terrible.'" Other remembrances suggest how resentful Nancy was that she had not received the premier education afforded for the only son Tom; sister Jessica shared that sentiment. Their mother endured the public humiliations; but by 1962, pushed to her limits, she told both Jessica and Nancy, "'I don't mind what you write about me when I am dead, but I do dislike to see my mad portrait while I am still alive.'" However, by then the Mitford family as a publishing enterprise had been firmly established.

Nancy's witty writing in the 1930s made her a popular party guest and provided her the financial freedom she craved. She could trade on her social connections for travels to the Cote d'Azur and other watering holes of the truly wealthy, acquiring more exotic color and droll in-jokes that her BYT friends could enjoy in her published works.

This glittering existence had its emotional dark places for her: though she enjoyed witty friends, she seemed unlucky in love. Hamish St. Clair-Erskine – to whom her first novel was ostensibly dedicated – resisted her overtures to marry him. Sometime after 1932 she attempted suicide, then joked that the act was "bad manners." Her rejection by St. Clair-Erskine lead her to make a hasty engagement to Peter "Prod" Rodd – and Rodd's proposal may actually have been a joke as she was reputedly "the third girl to whom he had proposed that week." Nevertheless, on December 4, 1933, she married Peter Rodd. Quite soon she recognized what would be her husband's lifelong habit of infidelity, even to his having an affair with her cousin Adelaide Lubbock. Urbanely, Nancy appeared to accept the situation, even vacationing in Brittany with Peter and one of his lovers.

Nancy desired to float easily on the social waters of her class, but the stirrings of war in the 1930s began to tinge her writing. Initially her political views on Socialism and Fascism were flippant, and her only interest in politics was for the funny commentary that she could spin for her social group. Her 1935 novel *Wigs on the Green* showed her customary skewering of her family by mocking sister Diana's marriage to beer heir Bryan Guinness and her sister Unity's fascination with Fascism. By 1939 Nancy finally acquired an experience that gave depth and commitment to her political views. Her sister Jessica had run away to join the Socialist fight in Spain against the Fascist leader Francisco Franco. The Mitford family sent the Rodds to Spain to coax Jessica into returning home. Although they were unsuccessful with Jessica, they were so shocked by the Fascist conduct of the war that they later traveled to France to help with the refugees from Spain. Nancy, finally observing the threat that Fascism posed to all of Europe, was truly sobered.

***

Pamela, born on November 25, 1907, suffered from poliomyelitis at age four, and so grew up to be quieter by comparison with the other members of her family. Like her sisters, she rode to the hounds, came out as a debutante, and had the requisite romantic entanglements and embarrassments that attended the Mitford girls. Unlike her sisters, Pamela did not publish about her family's life.

She became engaged to Oliver Watney of the famous brewing family; but the couple had second thoughts, printed an announcement in *The London Times*, and returned the engagement and wedding gifts—in itself a great public embarrassment for her family. Pamela did not return the engagement ring, but instead gave it to Unity who claimed that she later gave it to Hitler. Writer John Betjeman fell in love with Pamela and proposed twice to no avail. By the mid-1930s, though, Pamela had fallen in love again, this time with brilliant physicist, horseman, and married millionaire Derek Ainslie Jackson.

Derek and Pamela agreed to marry, and she moved in with him several months before his divorce was finalized. Jackson proved to be impressively inconstant as a husband: he would eventually marry six times and have multiple lovers. But for some years Derek and Pamela lived happily in Ireland. Unlike Nancy, she was always content with traditional country life, gardening, and taking care of farm animals. At one point she managed her brother-in-law Bryan Guinness's farm at Biddesden.

If Pamela had a noteworthy political moment, it occurred early in life when, as a true conservative aristocrat, in the General Strike of 1926 Pamela helped run a temporary canteen for strike-breaking truck drivers. She, like her siblings, traveled to Germany and met Hitler, whom she regarded as a rather ordinary man. As war approached, her husband muted his anti-Semitism and began work on scientific developments that could help the Royal Air Force.

Pamela, though, stayed sequestered at home, safe from the political waters roiled by other members of her family.

***

The sole Mitford son, Thomas, was born on January 2, 1909, and followed the educational trajectory of an aristocratic heir. He was sent off to boarding school by age eight where he had high placement as a bright student. While at Eton, according to James-Lees Milne, he developed his family-hewn wit into an engaging ability to win friends and lovers, both male and female. One of his best friends was Randolph Churchill, son of Winston. Tom visited the Churchills often at Chartwell; and, as other Mitfords also visited, Randolph developed a crush on Tom's younger sister Diana.

As he grew into a handsome ladies' man, Tom moved in the best upper-class circles. He skated with Olympic skater Sonja Henie; he charmed the journalist Sheilah Graham, later the lover of F. Scott Fitzgerald. He was also in the thick of many outrageous actions. One weekend was spent at Philip Sassoon's house with friends including Winston Churchill and T. E. Lawrence (of Lawrence of Arabia fame). Several of the men piled into seven small planes to fly over to see a friend, on the way startling people at Brighton and Littlehampton by buzzing the piers.

In 1927 Tom followed the path of many young privileged men and traveled abroad, ultimately to Vienna to learn German. Soon he traveled to Germany itself and fell so in love with the country that he committed to study law in Berlin. Like many English nobles, he considered that the Versailles Treaty had been somewhat unfair in its treatment of Germany, that Germany's move toward authoritarian government seemed a reasonable and a welcome antidote to social disruption and disorder, that movements such as England's General Strike of 1926 showed a rising threat from Socialism. Even Winston Churchill, when visiting in Italy, told Mussolini, "Externally your [Fascist] movement has rendered a service to the whole world' [in providing the necessary antidote to the Russian poison]." Churchill's views later changed; but at the time, he reflected a widely-held conservative perspective that Socialism was more disruptive of the working class, social order and government than was Fascism.

Tom Mitford, too, valued Fascism.

***

From her birth on June 17, 1910, Diana was a golden child always described as entirely charming and incredibly beautiful. In family friend James Lees-Milne's words, "'Divine isn't the word, for she was a goddess. More immaculate, more perfect, more celestial than Botticelli's seaborne Venus." She also shared the Mitford wit. As a teenager playing the organ at church, she made her own private joke by slowly improvising "Tea for Two" as a special piece. Diana's family's social connections would have always given her entrée into upper class society; but her wit and beauty carried her to the heights of British society.

In 1926 at age sixteen, Diana spent Christmas with her cousins the Winston Churchills at their country house Chartwell. The next month, she traveled to Paris with Winston and his son Randolph, who were on their way to Rome where Winston would meet with Mussolini and state his preference for Fascism over Socialism. The Churchill men accompanied Diana as far as Paris where she was to "'finish' her education and improve her French" as young aristocratic ladies were expected to do.

While in Paris, Diana's beauty attracted the attention of artists who enticed her to enjoy a social life that was outside the bounds of her parents' rules. She not only made exciting social connections but also became knowledgeable about Modern art and music. Reports of her unchaperoned escapades traveled back to her parents, who ordered her home and cloistered her in Devon for a length of time. However, the life, the art, the social whirl, and the political offerings of Paris would attract Diana and draw her to live in that city for most of her life.

In 1928, the year of Diana's official debut into society arrived. That spring, at age eighteen, she was formally presented to the King and Queen and emerged as the toast of society. Before The Season had concluded, she was engaged to the 22-year-old Bryan Guinness, "heir to one of the greatest fortunes in the country"; and their wedding on January, 30, 1929, was a premier social event that gathered all of the best families in the nation. Her bridesmaids included her cousin Diana Churchill. Upon wedding, the young Guinnesses were given an income of £20,000 pounds per year —the equivalent of $1.8 million per year in 2019 dollars.

Following a honeymoon in the Mediterranean, they divided their time among Bryan's various estates – Biddesden, an estate in Hampshire; Pool Place on the coast; and Knockmaroon, a great house in Dublin. But their London house at 10 Buckingham Street became the social hub of elite society that included the Cunards, Duff and Diana Cooper, Lytton Strachey, Dora Carrington, John Betjeman, Noel Coward, the Sitwells, and young Randolph Churchill. They were the Golden Couple of the highest social class in England. They entertained lavishly, were sought after for every party, and sparkled amidst an already-glittering social group. The Guinnesses easily traveled with their social set to Paris and other elite European watering holes, living the high life. A thinly-veiled record of the adventures of this social group was later recorded in Evelyn Waugh's novel *Vile Bodies*.

Despite such happiness, changes were coming for Diana that would alter her political views, emotions, and social connections. In 1930, the 20-year-old Diana bore her first son, Jonathan; and her selection of writer Evelyn Waugh and Randolph Churchill (Winston and Clementine's son) as his godfathers reveals that, at this point, she was still at the center of the upper-class social network. However, also in 1930, Bryan and Diana visited Tom Mitford at Berlin University. There they first heard the word *Nazi* and viewed the development of a new and highly-energized Fascist Party. Diana's newfound interest in Fascism soon brought her under the spell of Sir Oswald Mosley, leader of the British Union of Fascists. Mosley was wealthy, had impeccable social credentials, and was married to Cynthia "Cimmie" Curzon, daughter of Lord Curzon, the former viceroy of India. Mosley attended Sandhurst, fought and was injured during World War I, and became a Member of Parliament. Winston Churchill himself proposed Mosley for membership in The Other Club, "a dining club for men prominent in political life."

Mosley was also an unrepentant womanizer who had multiple lovers while married to Cynthia—a pattern of behavior that he called "flushing the coverts." He and Diana Guinness became lovers, but he refused to divorce Cynthia. Diana refused to lie to her husband; so, she divorced Guinness, and in January 1933 moved to 2 Eaton Square with her two Guinness sons, and lived openly as Mosley's lover. It was not Mosley's serial infidelities but the openness of Diana's move that proved scandalous within a social class that readily countenanced discreet affairs. Diana's parents would not allow her sisters to visit her at Eaton Square because she was now the mistress of the most infamous fascist in an England on the verge of war with Germany. It was only because Diana had such loyal friends that she was not entirely ostracized from her social circle.

The situation roiled even further when Cynthia Mosley died prematurely of peritonitis, which would have seemed to smooth the way for marriage to

Diana. Mosley instead chose to continue his affair with Cynthia's married sister "Baba" Curzon Metcalfe. Undeterred and resolved to wait for the return of her lover, Diana began to explore Mosley's Fascist interests by traveling with her sister Unity to visit their brother Tom in Germany. Because both Tom and Unity had social connections in Germany, they were given prime seats at the first Parteitag in Nuremberg. Other British travelers such as former Foreign Office worker Harold Nicolson and his son Nigel were present at this event that had, as its highlight, Albert Speer's Cathedral of Light display.

Diana eventually visited Germany four times in 1936 to seek German political support for Mosley to become prime minister in Britain. Her actions, though alienating some observers, still had not stepped beyond the pale of acceptable society at the time. In fact, after the 1936 Olympics, her cousin Winston Churchill invited her to talk with him about Hitler and to offer him her personal insights into the German leader.

During one of the 1936 visits to Germany – on October 6 – Magda Goebbels hosted the secret marriage of Diana and Mosley at the Goebbels' home. Hitler, Diana's sister Unity, and only a few others were present. The marriage remained a secret until 1938 when Diana became pregnant with a son Alexander who was born in November of that year. The revelation of this secret marriage caused great consternation and anger among her social set– Baba Metcalfe was utterly shocked – but Diana proved impervious to the criticism. She continued her travels to Germany, and in 1939 accepted Hitler's personal invitation to attend the summer Wagner festival at Bayreuth. This would be the last time that she saw Hitler. By September Britain had declared war on Germany, and both Diana and Mosley were imprisoned as threats to the security of the entire nation of Britain. The most beautiful woman in England was now the most hated.

***

Unity Mitford was born August 8, 1914, during the shock and patriotic zeal of the start of World War I. Her middle name, Valkyrie, seemed to foreshadow her affinity with those Teutonic warrior maidens and her headlong adoration of Adolf Hitler.

Unity's early years showed both her resistance to class expectations and a personal desire to be aloof, if not superior. An innocuous token of her aloofness was when she and her younger sister Jessica created a private language,

"Boudledidge," to allow them to communicate secretly in front of their parents. Though she achieved Nancy's goal of attending boarding school, she rejected the privilege and got herself expelled for "'a fine disregard of the rules of the school.'" Though attractive, she felt embarrassed by the difference made by her height of six feet, a worry that Nancy mocked in the Unity character of *Wigs on the Green*. Unity followed the traditional practice of her social class by coming out in 1932 as a debutante, but she seemed inclined to shock rather than to be witty as had been her sisters. She stole stationery from Buckingham Palace and sometimes carried a pet rat or a snake to dances.

Following the lead of her older sister Diana, she was attracted to Oswald Mosley's British Union of Fascists and began helping with the group when she could. The galvanizing political moment in her life occurred in 1934 when she persuaded her parents to allow her to spend a year abroad in Munich. While in Munich, Unity essentially stalked Hitler. She wrote to Diana:

> Such a terribly exciting thing happened yesterday. I saw Hitler… [A friend had phoned to alert her.] Of course, I jumped straight into a taxi, in which in my excitement I left my camera… . I went & sat down with them [her friends], & there was the Fuhrer opposite. The aunt said 'You're trembling all over with excitement', and sure enough I was, so much that Derek had to drink my chocolate for me because I couldn't hold the cup. He sat there for 1 1/2 hours. It was all so thrilling I can still hardly believe it.
>
> (letter to Diana, June 12, 1934)

She attended the second Parteitage in August and went to all possible venues where she could meet him. Eventually she settled upon a strategy of routinely coming to his favorite restaurant.

On February 9, 1935, Unity's stalking succeeded. Having noticed the repeated presence of this young woman with an attractive Aryan appearance, Hitler invited her to join him for a meal. Unity, smitten and star-struck, kept track of the 140 occasions she subsequently spoke with Hitler—about once every two weeks. They became such friendly companions that she was able to introduce her mother, Diana, Tom, and Pamela to him. American journalist Virginia Cowles gave this contemporary observation: "Unity was a tall Juno-esque girl, with shoulder-length blonde curls and large blue eyes. She worshipped Hitler with a school-girl passion and had persuaded her mother and father to come to Germany with her to see for themselves how wonderful he was." In Cowles's opinion, Unity saw National Socialism as "a Left Wing revolution and Hitler the champion of the downtrodden masses."

Cowles continued,

> Unity's brother, Tom Mitford, was a friend of mine in London and I had met the Redesdales before, so I saw them several times during the week. It was their first visit to Germany, and they treated the whole affair as though it were as detached from their lives, or the future of their country, as a bizarre operetta . . .. Lord Redesdale, a tall, handsome man with a large white moustache, wandered about with a bewildered air as though he were at a rather awkward house party where (curiously enough) no one could speak any English.

Hitler accepted Unity's adoration with affection, enjoying gossiping with her. At one party Cowles observed, "When everyone was seated Hitler's gaze wandered over the gathering and his eyes suddenly lit on Unity. His face broke into a smile, he nodded, and gave her the Nazi salute. She saluted back and a few minutes later Captain Wiedemann, Hitler's A.D.C., came over to our table and whispered in Unity's ear, 'The Fuhrer would like to see you. When tea is over, he would like you to come to his suite.'"

This relationship, beyond its friendliness, had public relations benefits for Hitler because he could present this daughter of an English peer at his rallies and have her photographed with him. As Germany became increasingly bellicose, these photo opportunities roused strong feelings back in England. Unity became increasingly at odds with her sisters Nancy and Jessica, who were more sympathetic to the socialist cause at this time. Nancy's novel *Wigs on the Green* (1935) may have mocked Unity's fascist beliefs, but Unity actually would make a Nazi salute before ordering in the local shop at Swinbrook.

Increasingly, Unity was a happily complicit participant in Hitler's publicity program. She wrote to a German newspaper declaring herself a "Jew Hater" and said that the English didn't understand the dangers that Germany faced. She became so notorious that when traveling with her family in Spain, Unity was physically attacked for wearing a Fascist badge. The British press opined, "'At It Again, the Mad, Mad Mitfords.'" Impervious to the criticism, Unity welcomed public opportunities to align herself with Hitler's cause, attending the 1935 Nuremberg rally with brother Tom and sister Diana and later attending the Olympic Games in Berlin in July 1936 as Hitler's personal guest. She rode to the 1936 Wagner Festival at Bayreuth in a car provided by Hitler. She twice visited Hitler's personal hideaway Berghof at Berchtesgaden. In 1937 British newspapers rumored that Unity—not Eva Braun – might marry Hitler.

Throughout the 1930s Unity felt an odd bifurcation in allegiances between home/England and Hitler/Germany, though she was increasingly becoming a *persona non grata* in England. On one hand, she attended the coronation of George VI; on the other hand, she wrote her sister Jessica that she would shoot Jessica's husband Esmond Romilly if necessary for the Nazi cause and would expect no less from him. She attended her sister Deborah's debutante ball and then returned to Munich where Hitler replaced her stolen swastika badge with two golden badges engraved with his signature.

Politically naïve, Unity was surprised when she was arrested for wearing a swastika in Nazi-threatened Poland. She was dazzled by flowers, photographs, and other gifts from Hitler, the man she idolized as "Wolf," utterly unaware or unconcerned that the gifts were perhaps taken from Jews.

Thus, it was not surprising that as war between England and Germany loomed on the horizon, Unity told her sister Diana that she would kill herself rather than choose sides.

***

Jessica Mitford, born September 11, 1917, also proved to be contrarian within her family and social set; though, rather than following the Fascism of Diana and Unity, she became enamored of Socialism with its rejection of social class and rank. Jessica felt allied with her two younger sisters against the older siblings who seemed too elevated to take notice of them. She developed a private language with Unity; and with Deborah she developed a private Society of Hens, who called themselves Hons and had a Honnish language. Like her sisters, Jessica attended dance classes and other expected social events. Her particular method of rebellion took the form of a truth-telling manner that often crossed the line into rudeness: as a nine-year-old at dance class she shocked her peers by explaining details to them about sex and childbirth. Her frankness, however, served her well on another occasion when she was experiencing an intense stomach pain, phoned the doctor, and requested to have her appendix removed. As it turned out, her diagnosis was accurate, and she later sold the offending organ to her young sister Deborah for £1.

Throughout her life Jessica seemed frustrated by her family and by her social class. Like Nancy, she felt she was denied a proper education and envied her cousin Sarah Churchill who was allowed to study drama. In 1929 she set up a "Running Away" account at her bank in which to save money for escaping her home. When she eventually was allowed to attend a small local private day school, she was not allowed to bring a friend home because Sydney did not know the girl's mother. Rebellion against her parents blended into rebellion against the class system. Jessica avidly read about hunger marches, economic depression, and fights between the police and strikers. For a brief time she joined a Sunbeam Club and naively sought to save a girl from inner-city life by having her come to live as a servant with the Mitfords. The unhappy girl soon asked to return home.

Jessica was deeply influenced by Beverly Nichols' *Cry Havoc*, a book describing the horrors of war and pleading for world-wide disarmament. She was also angered by her father's classist defense of the House of Lords: "May I remind your Lordships that denial of the hereditary principle is a direct blow at the Crown? Such a denial is, indeed, a blow at the very foundation of the Christian faith." She may have teased her father with the nickname "Sub-Human," but the teasing had a grounding in her true feelings of loathing of upper-class privilege and of her father's chauvinism.

While under the financial roof of her parents, Jessica alternately took advantage of her social position and then critiqued the privileges—a pattern that would characterize much of her adult life as well. She spent a year in Paris to polish her social skills for her debut. While in Europe she allowed Unity to introduce her to Hitler then railed at her family for failing to see the danger in the political policies that the Nazi leader espoused. By 1935 when she was presented as a debutante at the Palace, her sister Nancy mocked her as a "Ballroom Communist."

Not surprisingly, Jessica became enchanted with the romantic image cut by her Churchill cousin Esmond Romilly who at age eighteen had already been fighting with the Socialists against Franco in the Spanish Civil War. Mary Churchill Soames said that her cousins Giles and Esmond Romilly were "totally inappropriately known as 'the Lambs'"; it was probably coincidence that in 1932 the Churchills' Christmas tree caught fire while the Romillys were there. The firebrand Romilly boys, products of public school and privilege, readily used their ties to their cousin Winston even while lecturing him about his political views. Esmond's Socialist credentials predisposed Jessica to fall in love with him before she ever spent a day with him.

In 1936, her parents, worried by what they saw as her naive and possibly dangerous fascination with Socialism, attempted to distract her first by taking her to visit their Airlie cousins in Scotland and then by giving her money for what she told them was a tour in France with two cousins. She had lied to them. On February 7, 1937, David Mitford saw Jessica off for her tour of France. Instead, she took the money and headed to Spain to be with Esmond Romilly, whom she had actually known for only days. When news of her actions reached him, David was so angry that he vowed never to see Jessica again. Even though he lived for twenty more years, his farewell in 1937 was his last view of his fifth daughter.

Sydney Mitford once remarked, "'Whenever I see the words "Peer's Daughter" in a headline…I know it's going to be something about one of you children.'" Diana and Unity were already constantly in the news, but now Jessica made her own media splash: "Peer's Daughter Elopes to Spain." Young Mary Churchill, though she scarcely knew her cousin Jessica, "was very fond of Esmond. . . and so I followed the saga avidly in the press… [and] secretly I did think it tremendously dashing and romantic." At first, the family sent Nancy and Peter Rodd to try to get Jessica to return. Upon her refusal, they urged her to at least meet the social norm of marriage with Romilly. Jessica and Romilly did consent to marry, but Sydney was the only Mitford family member to attend their civil wedding in Spain on May 18, 1937.

The Romillys quickly found themselves in financial straits and so returned to London to live estranged from her family and among the poor whom their Socialist leanings embraced. It was a measure of Jessica's privileged naiveté that no one had ever told her that electricity had to be paid for. Ever contrarian, Jessica would visit rich friends and then steal things from them to sell to support themselves. At one point she and Romilly stole thirty top hats from Eton to sell.

Years later Jessica revised her assessment of Socialism, especially as it eventually spiraled downward into its destructive communist phase in Russia. She also experienced some early disillusionment, however, when her ideal of the "worker" jarred with the reality: the poor people among whom they now lived were the first actually poor people that Jessica had known personally, and she was shocked to see them as coarse. She became sobered about her plight when, in December 1937, she gave birth to a daughter who died of pneumonia after living only a few months. She and Esmond could no longer support themselves and literally hid from bill collectors. In such circumstances, a second pregnancy was unwelcome, and she decided to have an illegal abortion.

England offered little hope for them in terms of politics, finances, or family relations. Hence, when Jessica turned 21 in 1938, she collected her Running Away Fund and any inheritance she could have and the two emigrated to America. Ironically, it was the letters of introductions from upper class connections in England that gave the Romillys their first jobs in America and provided entrée into the upper-class social circles of New York and Washington, becoming friends with Katherine Graham, whose father owned the *Washington Post,* and Virginia Durr, a wealthy civil rights advocate and friend of Senator Lyndon Johnson.

Finessing their commitment to Socialism, they borrowed money from Clifford Durr and purchased a share of a restaurant in Miami, Florida.

***

The youngest Mitford, Deborah, was born March 31, 1920, at Asthall Manor in Oxfordshire. Like her siblings, Deborah's life seemed caught in the odd tensions of the Mitford economy. When Asthall seemed too expensive and large a house to keep up, it was sold; and "Sydney took all the girls to Paris on an 'economical trip' for three months." They moved to Swinbrook House, and David also purchased a Rutland Gate town house near Hyde Park in London. Swinbrook House became a beloved home for Deborah where she and Jessica would sit in the warm linen closet making rules for their "Hons Society."

Unlike her sisters who felt thwarted in their education and confined by their rural life, Deborah loved the outdoors, hunting, and country life. Her athleticism was natural and accomplished: she was such a good skater that "she was invited to join the British junior team" though her mother would not allow it. Dora Carrington, Lytton Strachey's lover and a friend of her sister Diana, praised young Deborah as a promising botanist who had "high spirits and charm."

Though her interests were rural and modest, parts of her young life seemed quite glamorous and momentous. She had entrée into upper class society and enjoyed visiting in such great houses as Castle Howard and attending the races at Royal Ascot. Despite the seeming economic stresses of her family, she was given a car for her 17th birthday; and she traveled to Italy, Austria, Switzerland, and Germany. She, too, met Hitler in June 1937 but was uninterested in him.

It was at an early age, too, that Deborah faced painful social exposure because of the passions and publicity caused by her siblings. When Jessica had eloped with Esmond Romilly, the media was so frenzied that some papers stated that it was Deborah who had eloped – an error for which she successfully sued them for £1,000. Esmond believed that Jessica should have had half of the settlement for having done the action. To avoid the notoriety caused by Jessica's elopement and marriage in 1937, her family felt that they needed to move Deborah's debutante year to 1938.

Deborah was not yet twenty when she had to accompany Sydney to Switzerland to bring home her Nazi-sympathizer sister Unity. Soon after, she would find herself the sister of the most-hated woman in England, Diana Mosley. Few young women could have coped well with such devastatingly bad public exposure.

***

The Mitford children were representative of many English aristocrats disbelieving that the arc of history was moving towards another war with Germany. It was safe to think that modern re-alliances were to be expected. So, Britain temporized when Hitler reoccupied the Rhineland in 1936, reasoning that the Versailles Treaty had perhaps unfairly divided Germany and placed excessive war debts and military restrictions upon the sovereignty of that country. They considered that it might be reasonable for Germany to claim large parts of native German-speaking regions—the Sudetenland—taken from Austria-Hungary at the end of World War I. At first the Spanish Civil War (1936-39) seemed another internal conflict between the strongman leader Franco and the socialists who opposed him until international powers became involved. In 1936 England itself had its own destabilization of government when the King did the unimaginable and abdicated in order to marry the twice-divorced American Wallis Simpson.

Political pressures increased when in 1937 German Ambassador von Ribbentrop stated that Germany must have "a free hand in Eastern Europe."

England still temporized. Only the most naïve person could have missed Hitler's manipulation to gain the *Anschluss (annexation)* of Austria in March 1938. Prime Minister Neville Chamberlain of Britain desperately sought to preserve "peace in our time" with his Munich Pact with Germany. It was only when Germany blatantly ignored national sovereignty and occupied Czechoslovakia in March 1939 that Britain and France felt drawn to guarantee Poland the protection through an alliance. On September 1, 1939, Hitler invaded Poland with impunity. Two days later, Britain declared war on Germany.

On the afternoon of Sunday, September 3, 1939, Unity Mitford walked into the English Garden in Munich, put her pearl-handled 6.35 Walther pistol to her head, and shot herself.

CHAPTER 13

KEEP CALM
AND CARRY ON

We may fail. But supposing we do not fail? ... I have always loved England. But now I am in love with England. What a people! What a chance!

Harold Nicolson
July 31, 1940

I'm very glad to be here. There is no place I'd rather be at this time than in England.

Gil Winant, American Ambassador to Great Britain
March 1, 1941

It was a terrible war, but if you were the right age. . . and in the right place, it was spectacular.

Pamela Digby Churchill Harriman
1994

When Britain declared war on Germany on September 3, 1939, the island's survival was not a certain conclusion. The lessons of The Great War had tempered any blithe enthusiasm about trouncing the Hun for fun and glory. America had withdrawn into a grim isolationism, resolved not to be drawn into a second "European problem." Meanwhile, German Panzers were inexorably crushing European countries under their tracks. Everyone watched as Ambassador Kennedy advised Americans to leave the sinking ship called Great Britain.

Not all Americans left. Janet Murrow, wife of the American journalist Edward R. Murrow, wrote her parents that she would not return to the safety of America: "'It just isn't possible for me to go off and enjoy myself when the world I have known over here is about to enter upon the darkest period of its history. I hope you understand.'" In fact, fortitude was perhaps the most salient resource left to British citizens watching their sons leave again for the continent. Unless one worked directly for the military or government, one was left with the uneasy task of attempting to lead a life normal enough to support the economy and, thereby, the troops. Given this scenario, how much of "normal" life was conscionable when troops were risking their lives?

Against this backdrop Winston Churchill achieved the highest aspirations of the aristocratic tradition to lead the nation to victory, earning his keep by forging the rough ore of homefront fortitude into a military virtue. His soaring rhetoric and dogged determination to rally the nation battled for Britain as powerfully as had his ancestors' use of horse and sword. The Battle of Britain may well have turned because of his words.

Aghast when Germany invaded Holland, Belgium, and France in May 1940, Chamberlain's government dissolved in panic and disgrace; and King George VI sent for Winston Churchill to become Prime Minister of a new government. Where most men would be daunted by the burden of facing the German juggernaut, Churchill would recall later, "'I was conscious of a profound sense of relief. At last I had the authority to give directions over the whole scene.'"

The entire arc of his ambitions and his career had led to this moment: to be the undisputed leader of the English government, the St. George who would slay the dragon and save the country, the hero in every aspect of the word. His enthusiasm and energy became overwhelming. He dictated to multiple secretaries at the same time, stayed up until the early morning hours, and directed action in dozens of departments of the government and military. Not surprisingly, he overwhelmed the War Cabinet with his tidal wave of ideas, directives, and absolute convictions regarding the conducting of the war. Soon he gained decisive powers over all actions. An unsympathetic observer might have argued that, though benevolent, "he became virtually a dictator" with control even over detailed military strategy. In a sense, he had reclaimed the right of his family and class to rule.

Perhaps Churchill's greatest strategic contribution to the war effort was to translate Britain's initial war failures and weak preparedness into Everyman's challenge to defend Albion, the island fortress. Three days after becoming Prime Minister, he vowed his dedication to the nation – that "I have nothing to offer but blood, toil, tears and sweat" – and the nation was irresistibly drawn to share his heroic vision of themselves as a nation called to an arduous challenge.

Circumstances immediately tested Churchill's capacity to take the tattered threads of an unmitigated retreat and to work them into this tapestry of mythic greatness he was weaving for his country. When the French Maginot Line of tunnels and bunkers failed to stop the German advance, English troops fighting alongside the French and Belgians were pinned with their backs to the English Channel and with divisions of Panzers advancing towards them. Only seventeen days after Churchill had assumed leadership, it seemed that the Allies would be slaughtered and the way cleared for a German invasion of England. Even the best estimates argued that only 30,000 of the 400,000 Allies could be evacuated in an unexpected pause of the German attack. Yet, in that brief window of opportunity, on Thursday, May 30, Operation Dynamo – the "Miracle of Dunkirk" – occurred. Nearly 800 fishing boats, yachts, ferries, merchant marine vessels crossed the Channel alongside the Royal Navy to bring the troops back home; and, by the end of the evacuation, over 340,000 had been saved.

Britons were exuberant at the collective effort that had saved their forces and maintained the island's protection. Although he reminded his countrymen that wars were "not won by evacuations," Churchill very astutely understood the opportunity to persuade regular citizens that they, too, were called, along with the military, to beat back the Germans. No histories of World War II can ignore the Churchillian speech that on June 4, 1940, hurled down the gauntlet to all Britons to meet the challenge as a roaring English Lion:

> Even though large tracts of Europe and many old and famous States have fallen or may fall into the grip of the Gestapo and all the odious apparatus of Nazi rule, we shall not flag or fail. We shall go on to the end. We shall fight in France, we shall fight on the seas and oceans, we shall fight with growing confidence and growing strength in the air, we shall defend our

island, whatever the cost may be. We shall fight on the beaches, we shall fight on the landing grounds, we shall fight in the fields and in the streets, we shall fight in the hills; we shall never surrender...

Churchill's island audience would almost immediately be asked to accept his grim promise that "We shall go on to the end" when Italy allied with Germany and the Nazis marched into Paris. By July 14 France had signed its separate peace with Germany.

The British Isles were now virtually alone in facing Germany, and on June 18 Churchill launched another verbal salvo intended to bolster his countrymen and serve notice to the United States that they, too, were not beyond the reach of Germany. In this speech to Parliament he gave the name to the aerial battle that was a fight for the island itself: The Battle of Britain (July 10, 1940-October 31, 1941):

> ...What General Weygand has called The Battle of France is over. The battle of Britain is about to begin. Upon this battle depends the survival of Christian civilisation. Upon it depends our own British life and the long continuity of our institutions and our Empire. The whole fury and might of the enemy must very soon be turned on us. Hitler knows that he will have to break us in this island or lose the war. If we can stand up to him, all Europe may be free and the life of the world may move forward into broad, sunlit uplands. But if we fail, then the whole world, including the United States, including all that we have known and cared for, will sink into the abyss of a new Dark Age made more sinister, and perhaps more protracted, by the lights of perverted science. Let us therefore brace ourselves to our duties, and so bear ourselves, that if the British Empire and its Commonwealth last for a thousand years, men will still say, This was their finest hour.

The Battle of Britain was fought in the skies over the country and also in the hearts of the civilians who suffered under the bombings, stringent rationing, and fear of full invasion. During these desperate months when Churchill was challenging the homefront to "keep calm and carry on," the United States thought that England could fall. Churchill also threw his powers of persuasion into wooing President Franklin Roosevelt into exchanging 50 aging US destroyers for 99-year leases on military bases in Newfoundland, Bermuda, and six other locations in the Caribbean. The gesture was a mere token from the United States; but Churchill's words caused the US to take a small, open, governmental step away from isolationism and, ultimately, towards alliance with Britain.

***

In the initial aftermath following Britain's declaration of war on Germany in 1939, the country had experienced no actual assault on its homeland. Frustrated by the anxiety of waiting for the action to begin, wags began to refer to it as the "Phony" War or the "Bore War." They joked about "Lord Haw-Haw" – the American-born William Joyce who broadcast German propaganda to the English. Resilience took many forms but maintaining normalcy seemed one of the most viable methods of thumbing one's nose at Hitler. Normalcy for the upper class meant sharing the dangers, emotions, and patriotism of the nation as a whole, but with every intention of maintaining its traditional distinctions. Lady Reading led the Women's Voluntary Service who, in green tweed suits and red sweaters, organized the evacuation of children out of London to host families in rural Northumberland and Cornwall, and would wait with tea and sandwiches to greet the evacuees from Dunkirk. The great houses would also play a part. Some such as Highclere Castle were outfitted as hospitals; others, for example Chatsworth, housed colleges or boarding schools. Even so, the wealthy began prudently to haul paintings, jewelry, and valuables to their country homes where they" threw 'house-cooling' parties" in defiant celebration. As the months progressed with no assaults, they drifted back to London and clustered with incoming foreign journalists at the Ritz, Savoy, and Dorchester Hotels.

This tension of war created relationships that pushed to early bloom in the hothouse of homefront London. Mary Welsh, *Time-Life* correspondent and future wife of Ernest Hemingway, saw the city as "a Garden of Eden for women in those years" with a "serpent dangling from every tree and street lamp, offering tempting gifts, companionships, warm if temporary affections.'" As Harrison Salisbury put it, "'sex hung in the air like a fog.'" After the American forces arrived in 1942, it was rumored that even General Dwight Eisenhower had an exceptionally close relationship with his driver Kay Summersby. Virginia Cowles — the American journalist who had reported with Ernest Hemingway during the Spanish Civil War and had borne witness at Guernica – observed, "No one wanted to be alone, however, and you heard respectable young ladies saying to their escorts: 'I'm not going home unless you promise to spend the night.'"

All Britons, though, felt the practical threat of invasion. Barrage balloons went up; sandbags and barbed wire surrounded Parliament. To avoid giving bombers flight reference points or targets, houses were blacked-out every night with windows boarded, curtained or taped. Directional road signs were taken down. There were fines for "lighting a cigarette in a doorway or holding a match up to read a road sign… Not since the Middle Ages had Britain been so dark." Iron railings were removed from buildings and melted down for guns. Churches could no longer ring their bells except to signal an invasion. Air raid wardens instructed their neighborhoods regarding procedures to follow during air raids, and citizens now carried identification papers and ration tickets for fuel and certain foods they could not grow themselves. The imagery of an imminent attack became even more frightening when citizens were issued gas masks and were required to carry them at all times.

Germany's invasion of Denmark and Norway in April 1940 signaled that Germany had vanquished these smaller threats and was now preparing to invade England. Cowles reported, "Even though the army slept with its boots on and the civilian population went to bed each night prepared to hear the church bells tolling to tell them the hour had come, no one had any fear as to the ultimate result. When you talked to the local inhabitants about it, they laughed and said: 'Let him try it.'"

Beginning on Saturday, September 7, 1940, and continuing every day until May 11, 1941, the German Luftwaffe mercilessly rained down bombs on the citizens of London. Nightly the wailing of sirens sent people running as instructed into air-raid shelters; crammed onto the platforms of the underground train stations; or, if caught out of a shelter, under a sturdy piece of furniture in a dining room. The night sky was lit up with flames from oil tanks exploding in the East End docklands. Batteries of antiaircraft guns coughed out bursts against the aerial bombardment while gunners dodged parachute mines and the shrapnel that rained down. Cowles reported that warehouses "made the greatest blaze. All night long they burned, millions of pounds worth of wool, tobacco, rubber and sugar fueling the most formidable fire London had seen since another September in the year 1666. Even where we were, forty miles away, the sky glowed pink." Edward R. Murrow transmitted from the tops of buildings, giving verbal pictures of the air raid siren he nicknamed "Weeping Willie"; of the fires that turned the moon "blood red"; and of the explosions that looked like "bursts of fireflies" in the night. Ten Downing Street and Buckingham Palace were hit by bombs.

The resilient bravery of the English became legendary during the Blitz:

> Each morning Londoners picked their way through the rubble and peered at the huge craters in the streets. John Lewis's department store burned to the ground, and many other London landmarks sustained damage, among them the Tower of London, the British Museum and the Tate Gallery. But the fortitude of Londoners was remarkable. 'The shops were full, old ladies sunned themselves in the park, and soldiers and their girlfriends strolled down Piccadilly arm in arm,' wrote Virginia Cowles. 'I lunched at the Berkeley restaurant and found it as noisy and crowded as ever.' When the United Service Club was hit by a bomb early one evening, members in dinner clothes stood transfixed as they saw through the smoke a naval captain standing at attention, a glass of port in his hand. 'Thank God that did not spill!' he exclaimed.

Murrow roamed through the city and returned to his broadcasts covered with dust and shaken by what he had observed. He described the "unsung heroes…those black-faced men with bloodshot eyes fighting fires, the girls who cradle the steering wheel of a heavy ambulance in their arms, the policeman who stands guard over that unexploded bomb." Reporter Ben Robertson reported how a cleaning lady had been "'three hours in the basement of her house…And she got to work this morning as usual.'" Bombed-out buildings in London had large signs saying, "BUSINESS AS USUAL." Cowles, covering a bombing raid on Dover, recalled meeting a girl in a shelter whose response to the bombing was "Christ, it's enough to ruin your digestion."

The upper class shared the general concern about where to sleep in safety. Guests at exclusive hotels such as Claridges would drag their mattresses out into the lobby, Cowles recording that "One night she 'tripped over King Zog's sister, who was sleeping peacefully outside the door of the Ritz restaurant." Lady Camrose refused even to use the bomb shelter just yards from her house because "any concession, however slight, was a moral victory for the Germans." By March 1941, "Dowagers unable to sleep could be seen in their robes, and knitting while dance bands played in the nearby ballroom [at Claridges]. 'From the general merriment you might have thought an enjoyable (if somewhat odd) costume party was going on.'"

The level of privation within the upper class at the beginning of the war was not extreme: "While ordinary citizens struggled with ration coupons to fill their larders, the kitchens at the Dorchester, the Ritz, and fashionable restaurants such as Mirabelle on Mayfair's Curzon Street were well stocked with strawberries and smoked salmon." Cowles reported that "The Rely on Us taxi service ferried young men and women through the blackout to the center of London nightlife, the Cafe de Paris, where Snakehips Johnson and his swing band played until 3:00 a.m. 'I found something strangely comforting in the placid, unruffled atmosphere… You felt that no matter what happened, London would always stand.'"

The Savoy Hotel "boasted one of the deepest, most luxurious shelters in town." American journalists began to gather there regularly. The British Ministry of Information representative, Douglas Williams, "moved his nightly briefings for the Americans to the bar, where he held forth, cocktail in hand." Some reporters such as Murrow felt somewhat embarrassed to be found amid the glitter and plenty of the Ritz and Savoy when working a news story about the city's devastation.

The carnage, however, was indiscriminate of class. Both Churchill's residence at 10 Downing Street and the King's Buckingham Palace suffered damage; and the bombing raids on April 17 and 18, 1941, killed over 2,000 Londoners. On May 10, 1941, incendiary bombs hit Big Ben, Parliament, and Westminster Abbey. Over 1,400 civilians died, 5,000 houses were destroyed, and thousands of fires burned for days. By that date the Blitz had claimed 43,000 lives.

In what were called the Baedeker raids, Hitler also intentionally targeted civilian cultural centers outside of London, most notably the medieval city of Coventry in the West Midlands, decimating 90% of its footprint. Nevertheless, the sight of American Ambassador Gil Winant and Prime Minister Churchill walking among the smoking wreckage miraculously worked to make people stiffen their resolve, clean up, and carry on.

Hitler finally broke his focus and shifted his priorities eastward to an invasion of Russia, essentially ending the direct assault known as The Battle of Britain.

CHAPTER 14

CAUGHT IN A MIGHTY WAKE: CHURCHILL'S CHILDREN

The journalist Virginia Cowles had been drawn to London in 1939 as a reporter covering the prospect of war as it first threatened to spill over from its hot boil in Europe. She became friends with Winston Churchill's son, "Young Randolph," even standing as godmother to Randolph's son. Her unusual access to the Churchills when they were in residence at Chartwell and at Downing Street, combined with her social and professional connections, gave her great exposure to the ways of the upper class in Britain just prior to the war:

> What surprised me most about these gatherings [in England] was that everyone seemed to have known everyone else since childhood. When they argued it was like a huge family wrangling among itself, each delighted to score at the others expense, yet underneath bound by a strong bond of loyalty. Opponents who crossed sharp swords politically played golf together over the week-ends; Chamberlainites and Churchillites made bridge foursomes, and the pro-Hitler Mitford family were cousins and friends of the pro-Churchill Churchill family [sic]. All in the grand manner: and '[a]fter an election the opposing candidates shake hands exactly as if it had been a game of tennis.'

Even with war looming, the London Season was still in full swing: "Everyone seemed determined to squeeze in the last ounce of fun before the war started," Cowles would note.

Hitler had taken Prague on March 15, 1939, but that summer Clementine Churchill still took her daughter Mary to Paris and to stay in Normandy with Consuelo Balsan, ex-wife of Sunny, 9th Duke of Marlborough. In August on the last weekend of peace, Randolph brought humorous playwright Noel Coward home to Chartwell for dinner. However, in wartime Britain, like many young English aristocrats, the Churchill children struggled to find their place in the socio-political world of a bombed-out London—and in its aftermath. Their case was exceptional in some respects because their father Winston cast such a long shadow; however, war meant that the comforting stability of upper-class traditions was challenged in all corners and that the historical social rules were in flux. Despite the advantages of wealth and connection provided by their noble families, the next generation of aristocrats struggled. The Churchill children in particular thrashed in a mighty wake; and in their personal lives, they struggled to stay on the surface.

The eldest Churchill child, Diana Spencer-Churchill, born July 1, 1909, grew up in the roiling aftermath of her father's Dardanelles disaster and her family's evacuation to the countryside to stay with their Romilly cousins Bertram and Nellie and their sons Giles and Esmond. Tiny and pretty, Diana – nicknamed the "gold and cream kitten" – showed all promise of a golden future. Like other young nobles, she attended debutante balls, often with her cousin and best friend Diana Mitford for whom she served as bridesmaid in 1929.

After her youthful social launch, Diana's confidence faltered. She briefly trained as an actress at the Royal Academy of Dramatic Arts but never chose to seriously pursue that career. She married John Bailey of South Africa in 1932 but divorced him after three years of marriage. Then, in helping her brother Randolph stand for Parliament in 1935, she met the man who defeated him, Duncan Sandys, whom she subsequently married in 1935. By the beginning of World War II, Diane was thirty years old; but as a mother of two with a third child due in 1943, she did not share the freedom of her siblings. Though she served with the Women's Royal Naval Service, Diana's family obligations meant that her prime minister father did not carry her along with him during his war service as he did with her sisters.

The end of the war primarily meant a return to motherhood for Diana, but her family life was haunted by her nervousness. She suffered several breakdowns, underwent electric shock therapy, and spent lengths of time in hospitals. Her marriage to Sandys could not stand the strain. They divorced in 1960 and she took back her maiden name. Several times she marshaled her strength to support her sister Sarah when she was in distress and volunteered with the Samaritans, a suicide prevention agency. Ironically, she died in 1963 from an overdose from barbiturates that was probably intentional. So, at age 54, the golden Diana was buried in the family cemetery in Bladon, England, near to Blenheim Palace.

***

Though not the eldest child of Winston and Clementine Churchill, Randolph Frederick Edward Spencer-Churchill (b. May 28, 1911) was the apple of Winston's eye, his "Chum Bolly" boy, the heir presumptive. At age eight he was sent to boarding school at Sandroyd and later attended the prestigious Eton where he became best friends with his cousin Tom Mitford. His math tutor at Eton made an observation that was to prove prescient about Randolph's life: he was "handicapped by his obsession for the sound of his own voice." With such a famous orator for a father, his aspiration to speechify was natural. He also inherited his father's love of a good fight, though he lacked his father's charm and subtlety in choosing and pursuing those fights. He was often mean-spirited and scrappy. Diana Mitford judged, "It would have been better if [Winston] had bashed Randolph [when he was rude to his mother Clementine], but he always let [Randolph] rip." Randolph's youngest sister Mary said, "'If he was in the right mood, he'd pick a quarrel with a chair.'" Randolph's erstwhile friend Evelyn Waugh once quipped, when Randolph had a nonmalignant growth removed, that "It was a typical triumph of modern science to find the one part of Randolph which was not malignant and then remove it." By his mid-twenties, Randolph began what would become a lifetime practice of suing – or being sued – for libel.

Young Randolph left Oxford without taking a degree to make money on a lecture circuit throughout the United States. The handsome young man made a great amount of money but spent most of it while in the United States. He then drew on his family connections to secure jobs as a correspondent for British newspapers such as the *Daily Mail* and the *Sunday Dispatch*. Regardless of his income, he gambled away so much money that he had to borrow against the annual £10,000 from his trust fund set up by his father Winston.

At the declaration of war, twenty-eight-year-old Randolph, charming when he chose to be and drawn to beautiful women, became focused upon marrying. His cousin Nancy Mitford wryly commented that his future wife "'was the 8th girl Randolph had proposed to since the war began, his best effort being 3 in one evening.'" That future wife was nineteen-year-old Pamela Digby, and he proposed to her on the first night they met. American writer John Gunther was startled because Randolph explained "in the presence of Pamela – that he was about to marry her because 'he must have a son and heir as soon as possible since he was convinced that he would soon be killed.'" They married in October 1939; wedding guests carried gas masks to the service.

Their child, born October 10, 1940, was the desired heir and was named for his grandfather, Winston. After this familial relief, Randolph returned to his army posting in Cairo where he was in charge of propaganda and censorship. Initially he was frustrated by not seeing action, but he enjoyed the luxury of living at the Shepheard's Hotel. As the war progressed, he did see active duty and achieved the rank of Major in his father's old unit, the 4th Queen's Own Hussars. His position as son of the British prime minister offered him the opportunity to mingle with ambassadors and major political figures. Once he boasted to American diplomat Averell Harriman of "'an affair I was having with the American wife of a senior British officer in Cairo.'" Ironically, later Randolph would angrily confront Pamela for having an affair with Harriman. Randolph and Pamela divorced in 1946.

Randolph's life after the war proved as contentious as had been his youth. Though always admitted into the high social circles, Randolph never attained the political standing that seemed his expected legacy from his father and grandfather. He was a Member of Parliament during the war but held no other public office during his lifetime. His career was spent in travel, journalism, writing, and almost continual litigation over libel accusations (both about him and by him). He married June Osborne in 1948 with whom he had one daughter, but he grew aloof from them both and kept to himself at his country home. Because of the international respect for Winston Churchill following the war, the project of writing his official biography was a plum desired by every historian. Randolph pushed and received the commission to write the biography. He had progressed only to the second volume before dying in 1968 at age 57.

***

Although only a Churchill by marriage, Pamela Digby (b. March 20, 1920) was an extraordinary example of an aristocrat adapting in the crucible of war and modernity. Pamela had, much like Nancy Mitford, grown up as a poor aristocrat who wanted the life that great money could provide. She traveled to Munich where she "coaxed Unity [Mitford] into taking her to tea with Hitler." Like other young debutantes, she was presented at court in 1938 and cleverly made social connections in dances and outings where she mingled with prominent daughters such as Rosemary and Kathleen "Kick" Kennedy, two of the American ambassador's daughters.

With her marriage to Randolph Churchill, she achieved two of her great desires: to have a great name and to be included in the most elevated social circles. Throughout her life she cultivated the practice of making herself useful – and irresistible – to powerful and wealthy men. She spent much time and care upon Winston Churchill, listening to his concerns about the war, playing his favorite game (bezique) for hours on end, relieving Clementine as hostess at many dinners. When she began her affair with the very wealthy, married, U. S. Lend-Lease administrator Averell Harriman, she became a back channel for U.S.-British negotiations. Not surprisingly, she remained welcome in the Churchill home while Randolph, who delighted in baiting and arguing with Winston, was less so. When she could no longer bear Randolph's arguments, Clementine banned him from the house until the end of the war.

Pamela had met Harriman in April 1941 at the luxurious Dorchester Hotel at a dinner party "in honor of Adele Astaire Cavendish, the sister of Fred Astaire and wife of Lord Charles Cavendish, son of the 9th Duke of Devonshire." Harriman, heir to the Union Pacific railway fortune and 49-years-old, had already been married twice, and was charming and good-looking. Even during times of strict rationing of food, "cases of Roederer Champagne, Chateau Margaux, gin, and Canadian whisky from the United States" and "such prized items as oysters, salmon, steaks, and whiskey" were served at his dinners. He paid for an apartment for Pamela and gave her an allowance of £3,000 per year ($230,000 in 2019 value).

When Harriman was reassigned to Moscow in September 1943, Pamela noted, "'I cried on Ed [Murrow's]'s shoulder and ended up in bed with Ed.'" When August 25, Paris was liberated in 1945, Murrow went over to report on the Allied takeover of the French capitol, and Pamela Churchill followed him. They may well have been at the Paris Ritz when Ernest Hemingway ordered fifty martinis for himself and friends to begin their celebrations. Later, Pamela followed Murrow to America as well where he was signing a new CBS contract. The affair ended abruptly with Murrow's telegram to Pamela: "Casey Wins." Janet Murrow had borne a son; and Edward, weighing that fact against his wartime romance, decided to stay with his wife.

From this point onward, Pamela would become, in one writer's words, "the greatest courtesan of the century." Pamela discreetly renewed her relationships with numerous rich and powerful men such as Elie de Rothschild and Fiat heir Gianni Agnelli before marrying the American theatrical producer Leland Hayward.

Averell Harriman, meanwhile, had been governor of New York and had made a failed attempt for president. By 1968, the now-widowed Harriman met Pamela at a Katharine Graham party in Washington, DC. Within months of Leland Hayward's death in 1971, Harriman married her. After Harriman's death in 1986, Pamela went on to become the U. S. ambassador to France and "was still serving as ambassador when she died of a cerebral hemorrhage in 1997, after a swim at the Ritz Hotel in Paris."

***

Sarah Millicent Hermione Churchill (b. October 7, 1914), like her cousin Unity Mitford, had been born at the beginning of World War I. Like her Mitford cousins, she was determined to live by her own lights: for good reason her nickname in the family was "the Mule." She did receive "finishing" in France; yet even as a 1933 debutante, she proved to be politically provocative, mocking the politics of her father's friends and earning a Socialist nickname, the "Bolshie Deb." Against her parents' preferences, she studied modern dance and acting. Similar to Jessica Mitford, in the summer of 1936 the red-haired, green-eyed, 21-year-old actress eloped to New York with a married actor, Vic Oliver, prompting London and New York papers to call her "the runaway debutante." Her brother Randolph was dispatched 24 hours later on the *Queen Mary* to stop the marriage but was unsuccessful. The couple married On December 24, 1936, after Oliver's divorce was finalized, and within hours returned to England. They were estranged by 1941.

Sarah turned to her father for a position in the Women's Auxiliary Air Force where she interpreted photographs for Operation Torch, the 1942 invasion of North Africa. A free spirit, she often traveled about the countryside on a borrowed army "motorbicycle." Later in the war her father had her serve as an assistant to him at the Allied conference in Tehran and at the 1945 Yalta Conference.

During the war, Sarah began a discreet affair with 51-year-old Gil Winant. Winant was no ordinary married man but the new U. S. Ambassador, replacing Joseph Kennedy. The handsome Winant was a "'gentle, dreamy idealist, whom most men and all women loved.'" Though he could have had luxurious food from the United States, he chose to live on British civilian rations. After most bombing raids, he walked among the ruins and made himself known as an American who supported the British people. Yet even Sarah's younger sister Mary saw that Winant had fallen "deeply in love."

The end of the war and Sarah's divorce from Oliver in 1945 brought the matter to a head. Winant offered marriage, but Sarah remained a free spirit, little interested in the institution at that point. By March 1946 Winant resigned as ambassador in hopes of being appointed secretary-general of the new United Nations organization. He attended the wedding of Mary Churchill but then returned to the United States in debt, disappointed at not receiving the UN job, and depressed by Sarah Churchill's rejection. On November 3, 1947, the man who had bravely endured the Blitz and staunchly advocated for the United Kingdom shot and killed himself at age 58. Londoners mourned Winant as a man who "was with us, up to the neck in our fight." Winston Churchill sent five dozen yellow roses to the funeral of this man who was the second American citizen (after Eisenhower) to be made an honorary member of the British Order of Merit. Sarah felt emotionally responsible for the death of her lover and would avoid mentioning of his name in her memoir, *Keep on Dancing*.

Sarah did turn to that rising theatrical power, America, for a steady career of stage plays, radio programs, film, and television. Sarah starred in *The Philadelphia Story* (1949), acted opposite Fred Astaire in *Royal Wedding* (1951), appeared on American *Hallmark* television programs, and returned to London to appear in a revival of *Pygmalion*. Amid her work in the United States, she met war artist and photographer Antony Beauchamp with whom she fell in love. Though her parents had never met Beauchamp, Sarah and Antony married at Sea Island, Georgia, in October 1949. Sarah claimed that she had sent cables to all of her family, but somehow none of the cables announcing this last-minute wedding arrived. Her parents heard about the marriage through the press before Sarah told them; Clementine "took it very hard indeed." The couple pursued their divergent careers and eventually were estranged. Antony Beauchamp overdosed with sleeping pills in August 1957.

By her own accounts in her 1981 autobiography *Keep on Dancing*, Sarah developed a drinking problem that caused her to be arrested for disturbing the peace on several occasions. News coverage of her arrest in Malibu, California, was widely publicized and led her to check herself into a clinic in Zurich. Still, her drinking problems dogged her. She attended wild parties and created great embarrassment for her parents. During the run when she was playing the lead role in *Peter Pan*, she was arrested in Liverpool. By 1961 she had accumulated probationary rulings that were finally enforced, and she "was remanded for ten days to Holloway Prison for a medical report."

After her release from prison, she caught the attention of Thomas Percy Henry Touchet-Jesson, 23rd Baron Audley. In April 1962, they married in Gibraltar. The next year he died of a massive coronary. In 1964 she became romantically involved with African-American jazz singer and painter Lobo Nocho, but then she left him to return to a career of peripatetic acting. Sarah died in London in September 1982, aged 67, and was buried near her parents and siblings at St. Martin's Church, Bladon, Oxfordshire.

***

Of all of the Churchill children, Mary Spencer-Churchill (b. September 15, 1922) hewed closest to the traditional conventions of her family and class. Essentially brought up as an only child, Mary adored the country life and benefited from that grounded life in her youth. At Chartwell she saw a good deal of her parents. Her memoirs contain homey stories such as her uncle Jack Churchill's ability to play the national anthem with his nails on his teeth. Her sister Sarah was near in age and affection; however, "Both Diana and Randolph were far too distant from me in age—being thirteen and eleven years my elder. . . I was always rather alarmed by Randolph, and I was gratified if they paid attention to me, they inhabited a different world, higher up the slopes of Mount Olympus—the world of grown-ups."

Her debutante year occurred during the Phony War when a modified Season continued in 1940 with Queen Charlotte's Annual Birthday Dinner Dance at the Grosvenor House Hotel. She breathlessly recorded the memory:

> In a time-honoured ceremony, after the dinner the "debs" of the year—the Maids of Honour—all in white ballgowns descend the great staircase into the ballroom, and advance towards the huge birthday cake with its appropriate

number of candles, which is then cut by the Dance president and Chairman, supported by her Vice Presidents: the ranks of debs then make a deep curtsy. After all this the dance gets under way and lasts into the small hours.

Even as late as May 1940 during the war, the Prime Minister's daughter was known to dance at the Savoy and return home by 4 a.m.

Though the royal presentation parties were canceled because of the war, Mary Churchill and her peers still attended the customary country house parties. At Petworth House, Mary was delayed in her first meeting with Lady Leconfield who was on air raid warden duty in the Park:

> So I waited, feeling shy and uncertain of myself, until suddenly the door burst open, and in came my hostess in her warden's getup: trousers encircled with bicycle clips, uniform jacket—and, swinging underneath the steel helmet surmounting her grizzled locks, the grandest and most beautiful pair of diamond pendant earrings I had ever seen in my life!

At first Mary seemed to share some of the wildness of her older sisters. About the Blitz, Mary recalled, "Whatever terrible things were happening, there were parties every night. Looking back, I am rather shocked that one night we went to a nightclub to find it had just received a direct hit and we just went on and found another." Her mother had to chastise her for coming in after 6 a.m. from a night on the town with friends. She impetuously accepted an offer of marriage from Eric, Lord Duncannon. At Clementine's request, Averell Harriman talked her into postponing the engagement and then ending an engagement she realized she didn't want. Aside from these few instances of impetuosity, Mary's behavior was impeccable in society's view.

By age 17, Mary began working for the Red Cross and the Women's Voluntary Service and served from 1939-1941. Initially she found it difficult being the Prime Minister's daughter in the Army: "I was received pretty frostily as everyone expected you to be above yourself. But once they discovered you scrubbed as many, if not more, floors as they did, they accepted one." She joined the Auxiliary Territorial Service helping with the gun batteries. Later she served as her father's aide-de-camp on the 1943 trip to Canada and the United States for the planning of Operation Overlord. For the rest of her life she would remember D-Day, June 5, 1944: " I seized a dressing gown and rushed down into the garden, and could just make out the forms of aircraft towing gliders thundering overhead: I fell to my knees and prayed as I had never prayed before." The nearly 850,000 Allied troops invading Normandy would mark the beginning of Germany's fall.

Mary continued her balancing of ATS service with her assistance to her father. As a guest of Charles de Gaulle, she accompanied her father to France on November 11, 1944, to celebrate Armistice Day. In 1945 she was transferred to Hamburg with her battery and was among the early witnesses to the liberation of the concentration camp at Belsen.

To the shock of a world who idolized Churchill for his wartime inspiration and leadership, in July 1945 the British citizens turned out Churchill's wartime government. What the world did not know was that Churchill was not really interested in domestic policy or governance and had few ideas for recovery after the war. As one Briton told Virginia Cowles, "'What's 'e know or care about babies' milk? Guns is 'is speciality and any time there's a war we're glad to let 'im run it but when 'e talks about babies' milk we know someone's put 'im up to it and it's not 'im speaking at all.'" Clementine, seeking to sooth her husband, suggested that "'It may well be a blessing in disguise.' To which Winston replied soulfully: 'At the moment it appears to be very effectively disguised!'"

In 1946, Mary still accompanied her father on a trip Paris where, at an embassy gathering, she first met Christopher Soames, an officer in the Coldstream Guards. After spending time together, he asked to marry her and she refused. His second effort proved successful; and they married on February 11, 1947, at St. Margaret's, Westminster, where her parents had married. She remained married to Soames until his death in 1987.

Mary's involvement in public life was far more tempered than that of her older siblings and yet quite forceful. She, her husband, and five children lived on a farm next to Chartwell. She aided her husband when he was ambassador to France, governor of Rhodesia at the time of its handover, and British Commissioner to the European Economic Community. Her independent accomplishments were many and included philanthropic work and publication of letters and materials related to her family's political life. She was made a Dame Commander of the Order of the British Empire and a Lady Companion of the Order of the Garter. Mary Churchill Soames died May 31, 2014, at age 91.

***

Although turned out from the Prime Ministership after the war, Winston Churchill persisted in asserting himself as a significant political figure. In 1946 he again used the power of his rhetoric to give the world a metaphor for the Communist threat by describing the walls constructed across Germany as an "Iron Curtain." In 1951 he made a charge and successfully won election as Prime Minister one final time. The awe and respect with which the new Queen Elizabeth II regarded him was a gratifying public recognition of his achievements as a national hero; the Marlborough line was again ascendant. A stroke in 1953 severely impaired Churchill's strength and ability to govern. He yielded to his designated successor, Anthony Eden, husband of Churchill's niece Clarissa. The succession had the feel of aristocratic legacy, but such was not the case. Eden's government was run by professional diplomats, bureaucrats, and politicians.

The changing times had financial implications for Churchill as well. At a time when Parliament ended the annual £5,000 pension "still paid by a grateful nation to the descendants of the victor of Trafalgar," Parliament offered no monetary grant to its war hero Churchill. Friends helped Churchill by purchasing Chartwell and allowing him to live there throughout his life; it was eventually deeded to the National Trust. His published writings and the assistance of admirers insured that Churchill would have whatever travels and entertainments he desired as he aged.

On January 24, 1965, Winston Leonard Spencer-Churchill died – seventy years to the day after the death of the man he sought to imitate and please, his father Randolph. Winston Churchill was 90 years old.

CHAPTER 15

"U AND NON-U": MITFORD WARS MOST PERSONAL

Winston Churchill's children represent the extreme case of young aristocrats whose socio-political connections allowed flexibility in "doing their bit" during World War II yet who struggled for postwar success in dealing with the legacy of their class heritage. Their Mitford cousins represented the other aristocratic extreme dealing with class heritage while living out the war, primarily on the homefront. Their childhood weaving of affection and belief frayed in their adult, very public, battles over politics that proved so vicious that one could well wonder whether any family could survive such intense emotional grievances so largely self-inflicted. These family battles fought in front of their class and in the widest media coverage reflected fissures among the nobility at large. Socially and politically, the public indiscretion of Diana's affair with a Fascist, Jessica's elopement with a Socialist, and Unity's public endorsement of Hitler flouted class taboos regarding discretion, tradition, and patriotism. Their behavior provided reinforcement to any opponents that this privileged class had long outlived any usefulness that it may have once had in prior centuries. With increasing threat, many asserted that an accident of birth should not shower such wealth and status upon people so at odds with the public good.

Sydney and David Mitford initially tried to follow after their offsprings' political interests but ultimately became estranged from each other under the strain. Both Sydney and David had met Hitler; and Sydney—wanting to support her children's passions—conceived a sort of forgiving fondness for him. For David, though, once Germany was the enemy of Britain, he could never tolerate the man or his country. What bedeviled both parents was that they shared the commonly-held conviction of their generation that "the name of a decent woman should appear in the newspapers only twice: first on her marriage, and second in her obituary." Such was not the case with any of their daughters. Their actions so painfully tested David's patience and heritage, he simply withdrew from the family battle. In 1938 he had purchased Inch Kenneth, a Scottish island. He moved to the island and spent the next twenty years there, separated from his wife, isolated from his children, no longer wanting to witness the erosion of the traditions and heritage with which he had grown up. He died there in 1958; Sydney survived him by nearly five years.

Inch Kenneth was isolated; yet – with 30 hours of travel by train, car, boat, ferry, and cart – technically accessible. It was an apt symbol for the relationship among the Mitford children as they made their ways through World War II and into a world that badgered them for their personal stories.

***

Nancy Mitford seldom missed an opportunity to skewer her family in her fiction and to toss it off as humor. Her pre-war *Wigs on the Green* had mocked Unity's fascination with Hitler. In *Pigeon Pie* she wrote a thinly-veiled record of Diana's affair with Oswald Mosley, posing it as a story about the social swirl of socialite Sophia and her Hitler-admiring husband. Once armed conflict with Germany began, Nancy's family bitterness found a patriotic face. She secretly went to the Home office and denounced Diana as a traitor under Defense Regulation 18B of the Emergency Powers Act, which suspended the right of habeas corpus and gave the British government power to detain German sympathizers who might cause trouble.

Though she was popular and happy within her social set, Nancy's personal life faltered. When the war began, she opened the Mitfords' Rutland Gate house in London to the homeless; but she lost energy for the cause and closed it. Her husband Paul's open infidelities eventually so hurt her that she briefly took a French lover, Roy Andre Desplats-Pilter. Her income from writing dwindled in the wartime economy; so, in March of 1942 she took a job at

Heywood Hill's bookshop. Since she had serially alienated her family through her writing, her relationship with them remained prickly and tenuous.

Almost as a force of will, Nancy selected one man to whom she would cling and upon whom she would lavish her love for the rest of her life. In September 1942 at a party, she met Charles de Gaulle's Oxford-educated, socially well-connected Chief de Cabinet, Gaston Palewski. Palewski was charming, witty, and soon became Nancy's occasional lover. He never requited with fidelity, but she dedicated herself to him for the rest of her life. Inspired, she wrote another semi-autobiographical novel, *The Pursuit of Love*, in this case, immortalizing her lover as the character Fabrice de Sauveter. Published in December 1945, the novel became an instant best seller and finally established Nancy as a popular, financially successful writer.

When the war ended and he returned to Paris, Nancy followed, bought herself an apartment in Paris, and devoted herself to Palewski even after he married Duchess Helen-Violette de Talleyrand-Périgord. The postwar Paris of 1946 also suited Nancy's desire for a social circle that was witty and wealthy. Her friends included Lady Diana Manners Cooper, wife of the British ambassador; Daisy Fellowes, mistress of Diana Cooper's husband, Duff Cooper; Violet Trefusis, daughter of Edward VII's mistress and lover of Vita Sackville-West. Her continuing publication successes allowed her to indulge her passion for dressing fashionably, opining that "being well-dressed was a matter of health." The only spoiling element was that her estranged husband Peter Rodd continually asked her for money, stopping only when she forced him to agree to divorce her in 1957.

In 1949 Nancy again tapped her background for source material in *Love in A Cold Climate*, a humorous view of the English upper class. However, the work that made her a cult hero was a slight essay she wrote for a collection entitled *Noblesse Oblige* entitled "U and non-U" (1956). In this essay, which she claimed was a joke, she identified the characteristics of the upper class ("U" or "Us") vis-a-vis the lower classes ("non-U" or "not Us") with a sardonic humor that entertained her friends and became a model for imitators. Such publication and publicity allowed her to live the rest of her life on her laurels as a wit and raconteur.

In the 1970s she was diagnosed with a malignant tumor on her liver and then with Hodgkin's Disease. In a cruel irony, her sister Diana, also living in Paris at this time, cared for her during her lengthy illness, not knowing until after Nancy's death of Nancy's wartime denunciation that helped cause such suffering for Diana.

Nancy's death on June, 30 1973, finally brought her home to Swinbrook, the home she hated, and to the churchyard where her sister Unity was buried. In a final satiric thrust at her family, she directed that the Mitford family emblem, a mole, be carved on her tombstone.

***

After the war, Pamela Mitford Jackson was divorced from her husband and received enough wealth from her divorce settlement to live independently, most often in Switzerland and in Gloucestershire. Pamela became good friends with her ex-husband, Derek, and with his various wives, but for nearly forty years her companion in Switzerland and for many of her travels was female companion Guiditta Tommasi. Pamela was content in her life, a "serene" person who enjoyed raising chickens, spoiling her pet dachshunds, and delivering odd humorous memories of the past. She never engaged in the family enterprise of autobiography, though she would entertain family and friends with her memories of great dinners and adventures from their youth. One well-loved story was about their father bringing a small pony into his train cabin: she always concluded with the observation that "'Of course it was most unusual for ANYONE to travel 3rd class in those days.'"

In April 1994 Pamela visited friends in London for a weekend of shopping and dining. On Saturday night she fell down a steep stairway and broke both of the bones in her right leg. She seemed to be recovering, but a blood clot developed and by Tuesday morning she had died, ten minutes before Deborah arrived from Ireland to visit her. She, too, was buried at St. Mary's Church cemetery at Swinbrook with the epitaph "Valiant Heart" on her tombstone.

***

When war finally came, Tom Mitford joined the British forces and in 1942 was posted to Libya. In 1944 as the Allies began to close in on Germany, Tom could not bring himself to fight in Germany itself, a country he had come to love. Using his social influence, he had himself posted to the Pacific Theater of Operations. His transfer took him to Burma where, while leading a force against a small group of Japanese, he was hit by machine gun fire. A bullet to the spine caused paralysis; and six days, later on March 30, 1945, he died of pneumonia at age 36. He was buried in the military cemetery near Rangoon.

At his death the family title and fortunes went to Tom's uncle, his father David's younger brother.

***

Hitler's war cost Diane Mitford Mosely and her husband Sir Oswald Mosley in both status and personal suffering. Even though Diana's husband avowed his support of England, his fascist views identified him with Hitler. Under Regulation 18B, Mosley was imprisoned on May 23, 1940. With the support of sister Nancy's denunciation, Diana, once the center of London social life, was imprisoned as well and became regarded as "the most hated woman in England." When Diana's cousin Winston Churchill—now Prime Minister – contacted sister Jessica to report that he was trying to ease conditions for Diana in Holloway Prison, Jessica told him frankly that Diana and Mosley should be shot. She demanded that Churchill not release the Mosleys or give them clemency. In the public eye, perhaps it was Diana's patrician attitude about the matter that irritated in equal measure with her support of her husband's politics. While in prison, she used her Harrods charge account; and the press used such instances to suggest that her imprisonment was cosseted. In fact, this couple, who had not been charged with a crime, did have to endure most of the deprivations experienced by their prison mates. Diana remained in Hollowell Prison or under house arrest for 3 ½ years.

Eventually, the imprisoned Diana called upon her family connections to gain relief for herself and her husband who was suffering from phlebitis. She viewed her cousin Winston Churchill as responsible for this unfair imprisonment and disdained petitioning him. Still, Winston's wife Clementine had been a bridesmaid at her parents' wedding, and Diana Churchill had been a bridesmaid in Diana's wedding to Bryan Guinnesss; and so, she relented enough to ask her mother to importune Clementine. Winston Churchill readily effected a change that allowed Diana and her husband to be interned together at Hollowell Prison. By November 1943, Churchill arranged that the couple be released and stay under house arrest at a country home. Public protests against Churchill's actions were loud and angry, but he withstood them and the Mosleys lived quietly and reclusively under house arrest until August 1945.

As soon after the war as they were permitted their passports, the Mosleys left England. Oswald Mosley still had great private wealth, and so they traveled in Europe and eventually lived in Ireland for over two years. Their final home became Le Temple de la Gloire near Paris. Ironically, they were neighbors to another couple who had actually been banished from England, Edward VIII and Wallis Simpson, now the Duke and Duchess of Windsor. Mosley never regained political power despite his lifelong efforts to do so. He developed Parkinson's disease and died in 1980. His ashes were scattered in the garden of their home at Orsay.

Diana never learned the depths of Jessica's animus and did not until after Nancy's death know of Nancy's complicity in her imprisonment. Accordingly, her autobiography, a *Life of Contrasts* (1977), offered a kind view of her family and her marriage to Mosley, whom she unfailingly defended. Among her other writings were a biography of the Duchess of Windsor (1980) and *Loved Ones* (1985), a book of memories of famous friends.

Diana remained a beautiful woman even in old age; she maintained happy relationships with her children. Two health problems beset her: throughout her life she suffered from migraine headaches; and for the last twenty years of her life her hearing deteriorated into almost complete deafness. She lived to be 93, dying on August 11, 2003. Even in death her beauty was celebrated by an obituary that called Diana "The Fascist Who Dazzled." She was cremated and buried next to Unity's grave in the St. Mary's cemetery at Swinbrook.

***

At the beginning of the war, Unity Mitford had shot herself, but the wound – though grave – did not kill her. For some time, she remained in a coma; and, when she awoke and realized her failure, she again attempted to kill herself by swallowing her swastika badge. Her brain injury gradually affected her reasoning capacity to the extent that such attempts ended. Still, Unity's treatment and recovery remained a question, and it was a measure of Hitler's fondness for her that he paid her medical bills and arranged to have her taken to the neutral country of Switzerland from which she could be transported to England.

Unity's suicide attempt would have been a propaganda nightmare, and so Hitler banned the German press from reporting it. Hence, Unity's anxious family had received no firm word about her well-being or whereabouts after the beginning of the war. In late December 1939 they received a phone call from Switzerland, where Unity herself weakly told them that she was ill and wanted to return home. Quickly Sydney and nineteen-year-old Deborah packed and left on the treacherous journey through wartime Europe. When they finally arrived, they found Unity to be in terrible condition: her hair was matted, and she seemed frail and disoriented. With little time to prepare, they arranged transportation and left on a perilous return journey exacerbated by Unity's pain. Worse circumstances awaited them. The press had caught wind of this mission to return the Nazi-lover to England, and they confronted the travelers at Calais. The press coverage was brutal, not only because Unity was a protégé of Hitler, but word leaked out that the cost of bringing Unity home was £1,600, over three times the cost of a three-bedroom house in 1939 England. The public was outraged, and the family had to keep Unity secluded both for her health and for her safety. While the wound had not proved fatal, it rendered Unity an odd shell of the lively, passionate young woman she had once been.

Unity's return forced a final rift between her parents. David would have nothing to do with her care, and Sydney had to dedicate her life to taking care of this daughter who had mentally regressed and was physically incontinent. Dependent and limited, Unity lived a diminished life until she died of meningitis on May 27, 1948, just a few years after the death of the German fascist who had attracted her from her family, class, and country.

She was buried in the St. Mary's cemetery at Swinbrook. Her epitaph reads: "Say not the struggle naught availeth."

***

At the start of the war, the ostensible Socialist, Jessica Mitford Romilly, was working at a Miami restaurant that she and her husband Esmond partly owned. Esmond felt the call to rally to England's support and joined the Canadian Royal Air Force. They sold their stake in the restaurant, and Jessica returned to Washington, D. C., where she lived for 2 ½ years with civil rights activists Clifford and Virginia Durr.

On November 30, 1941, Esmond was listed as missing in action in Europe and later declared dead. When Winston Churchill, visiting in the United States, offered Jessica his condolences and a gift of financial assistance, she snubbed both. Now 25 years of age, a widow, and needing a job, she lied about having a college degree to secure a job with the United States government. While working in Washington, she met and fell in love with a Jewish lawyer, Robert

Treuhaft. When Jessica's job transferred her to California, Treuhaft followed her and proposed. They married on June 21, 1943.

In 1944 Jessica became an American citizen and openly a member of the Communist Party. The McCarthy investigations of the 1950s meant that any avowed Communist would be under suspicion; and so, not surprisingly, in 1951 Jessica was subpoenaed by the California State Committee on Un-American Activities. She literally hid from authorities for several years in order to avoid further subpoenae. By 1956, the revelations about Stalin's murder of Russians caused Jessica to become disenchanted with Communism, though she remained an advocate of Leftist causes. At great personal risk, she worked in Alabama and Mississippi to register voters and advance the goals of the civil rights movement.

Writing under the name Jessica Mitford, in 1963 she finally published a book that would bring her fame and financial success. The book was *The American Way of Death,* an exposé of the unethical practices of the funeral industry, contending that funeral directors sentimentalized death to take advantage of grieving families in order to make excessive profits from the sale of services and products. When she was interviewed on television and radio, her Mitford wit made her a memorable personality. She remained a firebrand and a contentious figure throughout her life, protesting for civil liberties and befriending controversial figures such as the writer Salman Rushdie.

Jessica maintained prickly, if not bitter, relations with the rest of the Mitford family throughout her life. Even after two decades, Jessica never reconciled with her father. When he died, David bequeathed his Scottish island to all of his daughters except Jessica; and, though her sisters chose to include her in this inheritance, Jessica wished to sell her part and donate the money to the Communist party. She barely tolerated seeing Diana when visiting the dying Nancy; and over fifty years after her elopement, she contacted Diana only a few times. In 1976 Pamela, Diana, and Deborah disapproved of David Pryce-Jones's biography of Unity and of the inclusion of anti-Mosley letters in television interviews about the family; through such letters, Jessica attacked her sisters calling them "snide" and "foul." When Deborah attempted to smooth the waters and establish family rapport, she bitterly asked, "Why should you be the final arbiter of everything about the family?" She did visit Chatsworth for the wedding of Deborah's daughter but otherwise visited little with Pamela and Nancy and none with Diana. For over a decade she sparred with Pamela and Deborah who had mistakenly thought she had taken a family photograph album from Chatsworth. Despite this acrimonious estrangement, for much of her life Jessica readily traded on her family's name and connections. She used the Mitford name in all of her publications; she never hesitated to draw upon social connections when she had need; and she, like Nancy, felt no compunction about airing her family history. Her memoir entitled *Hons and Rebels* (1960), a reminiscence about the Mitfords' childhood, seemed inaccurate to her siblings and an unkind portrait of their mother as incompetent.

A heavy drinker and smoker throughout her life, Jessica developed cancer of the brain. Throughout her painful struggle with disease, her daily visitor until her death on July 22, 1996, was her friend, poet Maya Angelou. In keeping with her views regarding the funeral industry's exploitation of death, Jessica received an inexpensive funeral with little ceremony and had her ashes scattered in the Pacific Ocean.

***

Britain's isolated position at the start of the war had galvanized everyone. Even George VI's Queen prepared to do her bit: she told Harold Nicolson that she was being "instructed every morning how to fire a revolver. I [Nicolson] expressed surprise. 'Yes', she said, 'I shall not go down like the others.'" Passions ran high among young people who couldn't be certain from day to day of surviving the blitz at home or the battles abroad. It was not surprising, then, that at a dinner party Deborah met and soon fell in love with Andrew Cavendish. Andrew's older brother, William "Billy" (Lord Hartington), was to inherit the title and lands of their father the Duke of Devonshire. As the second son, Andrew's prospects would be secure, well-connected, but not especially wealthy by the standards of the class. Nevertheless, swept up in the uncertainty of war, Andrew and Deborah decided not to wait for the war's end in order to marry. The wedding they had on April 19, 1941, was a mix of grandeur and wartime exigencies. The Devonshires invited 500 guests but had none of the pages or bridesmaids customary in a grand wedding. Deborah had a wedding gown made from 80 yards of white tulle, but her father gave her away in his Home Guard uniform. The couple had a cake but no icing since sugar was rationed.

For her, this marriage into an undeniably prominent upper-class family brought Deborah into an even broader international social stratosphere. Andrew's uncle Charlie Cavendish was married to Adele Astaire (sister of the famous dancer), and his uncle Harold Macmillan was a future Prime Minister. During the war Andrew's brother William met and became romantically involved with Kathleen "Kick" Kennedy, daughter of Joseph Kennedy, the United States Ambassador to Britain. Deborah and Andrew came to know all of the Kennedys well, a social connection that later brought invitations to John Kennedy's inauguration and funeral in the 1960s.

Although the Devonshires were socially prominent, the Kennedy parents opposed the marriage of William and Kathleen because the Devonshires were Protestant—and possibly because Joe Kennedy did not want his daughter living in a country that he had predicted would be conquered by Germany. After a lengthy courtship and despite the opposition, the two married May 6, 1944, making Kathleen the future Duchess of Devonshire. Barely four months later, on September 13, a sniper killed William. Churchill had 24-year-old Kathleen flown to the Devonshire country house Chatsworth for the funeral. Kathleen, now reduced in rank to Lady Hartington, bought a Georgian town house in London and, after a period of mourning, continued a lively life there. Among her friends was Pamela Churchill with whom she sometimes vacationed.

After the war, Pamela Churchill and Kathleen often traveled to France together and in 1947 stayed at Lismore Castle, a castle in Ireland owned by the Devonshire family. By 1948 Kathleen Kennedy Cavendish had fallen in love with Peter Fitzwilliam. In May of that year Pamela Churchill accompanied Cavendish and Fitzwilliam to Croydon Airport and saw off the lovers as they left in a small private plane to fly to Cannes. Midway in their flight, the plane was caught in a thunderstorm and "crashed into a mountain ridge north of Marseilles." The pilot and passengers all died. Kathleen Cavendish was buried in the Devonshire section of St. Peter's Church cemetery on the Chatsworth estate.

The death of William Cavendish meant that Andrew and Deborah would now be the future Duke and Duchess of Devonshire. Their management of Chatsworth in postwar life represents one of the best cases of survival of a great house and a great family into the twenty-first century.

CHAPTER 16

CHATSWORTH AND
THE CHATELAINE

When Edward Cavendish, the 10th Duke of Devonshire, died unexpectedly of a heart attack at age 55 on November 26, 1950, one could understand a family's grief. However, times had changed since the passing of the 9th Duke and few ordinary citizens would appreciate the potential financial ruin this untimely demise caused the Duke's 30-year-old son Andrew and his wife Deborah Mitford Cavendish who were now set to inherit title and estate.

The wartime death of eldest son William in 1944 had unexpectedly made Andrew Cavendish heir to the Devonshire title, a status which—whether he and Deborah wanted it or not—would encumber them with debt and properties as well as unalterably fix nearly all of their life choices. The young couple had anticipated decades in which to prepare for the obligations of title and land ownership; but their preparation time abruptly ended, and they had to confront the financial assaults, the most pressing being the disaster embodied in Lloyd George's "death tax."

If the 10th Duke could have gradually made over his estate to Andrew and lived for five years after transferring that property, much of this heavy tax could have been avoided. Edward had indeed begun this transfer in 1946 when he was 51 years of age; at age 56 he would have freed his son of a tremendous burden.

His death just fourteen weeks short of the deadline opened an economic abyss for his son and daughter-in-law.

The tax bill was set at the full rate: 80% of everything the Devonshires owned, well over $300 million in 2019 value. The reason for this astronomical tax bill was that the Devonshires owned – among other properties – Lismore Castle in Ireland; Bolton Hall in Yorkshire; Compton Place in Eastborne; Hardwick House, Edensor House and Chatsworth in Derbyshire; 120,000 acres of land; and masses of valuable paintings, tapestries, furniture, jewelry, and art pieces. In addition, the interest on the taxes accrued at the rate of £1,000 *per day*. Although few ordinary citizens would sympathize with such a wealthy couple, Andrew and Deborah faced catastrophic loss because their wealth was bound up in material assets, not in cash. In order to have money to pay such a bill, the new 11th Duke and Duchess of Devonshire would have to try to sell a great deal at a time when England's post-war economy was still so weak that a reasonable profit could not be made.

Aside from the tremendous tax issues, the young Duke and Duchess faced the very practical and demanding requirements of maintaining the properties and the art objects within their country houses. Chatsworth alone had one and a half acres of roof to maintain. Who could restore frescos or stored oil paintings – and how would that be paid for? What crops or farm business would be profitable in post-war England? How much staff was necessary and affordable? Because their holdings were vast, these questions required answers that differed according to location, condition of the house, and state of the labor force. The restoration and management strategies employed at Chatsworth illustrate the savvy adaptations required to maintain a stable estate that could withstand the threat of decimation by taxation.

Chatsworth was a country estate that attractively blended nineteenth century industrial innovations with classical garden design. It gained renown in the nineteenth century for gardens remodeled by Joseph Paxton, later the designer of the Crystal Palace. Between 1832 and 1836, Paxton erected greenhouses, orchid houses, planted an arboretum, and built the largest rock garden in the country. Embracing the industrial innovations of his age, Paxton "designed and installed the famous Emperor Fountain, which could send a jet of water 290 feet into the air—a feat of hydraulic engineering that has since been exceeded only once in Europe." The Duke was so enthralled with Paxton's grand concept of garden beauty that he tore down and moved "the estate village of Edensor because some of its cottages spoilt his view from the house out over the parkland."

Along with John Marples, Paxton designed and built a conservatory that was certainly a prelude to the Crystal Palace: "276 feet x 123 feet—big enough to contain a small football field. The vast spanned arched roof was supported on iron pillars and curved to a height of 57 feet. This framework was filled with 70,000 square feet of glass, and it took four years to erect." It allowed Paxton's employer, the 6th Duke of Devonshire to house his worldwide collections made as a plant hunter.

As would become true of many great country houses, such grand designs could be sustained only so much. During World War I the fuel ration did not extend to heat the conservatory, and so the tropical plants all died. The conservatory itself, now bereft of its original purpose, was demolished in 1923. The family home in London, Devonshire House, site of the spectacular ball in 1897, was razed after World War I and replaced by a branch of the Marks & Spencer department store chain. During World War II Penrhos College had occupied Chatsworth, and great repairs had to be undertaken to return the house to a usable condition after the college left.

Upon inheriting the death duties in 1950 that came with the title of 11th Duke, the Devonshires set out the save Chatsworth. To do so they sold 12,000 acres of their estate in Dumfriesshire; 42,000 acres in Derbyshire, property in Sussex, a house in London; nine paintings by Rubens, Holbein, Rembrandt, Van Dyck; and 141 precious books. In 1959 they also deeded over the large and architecturally significant Elizabethan structure Hardwick Hall to the government.

In the midst of multiple financial crises, Deborah came into her own as a practical, resilient chatelaine. To a great degree, she was the person who urged the revenue-increasing expansion of visiting hours and visiting opportunities at the estate; the establishment of agricultural ventures; the sponsorship of riding competitions; and the development of educational programs based upon Chatsworth's art, gardens, and architecture. She developed "Duchess of Devonshire" as a brand and a business that produced agricultural products for sale throughout the country. In addition, the Devonshires became successful owners of various Devonshire Arms hotels and restaurants throughout the district. Most importantly, the Duke and Duchess developed a Chatsworth Trust designed to protect the estate assets from crippling taxation for the foreseeable future. Yet, despite these vigorous efforts to pay the taxes, the debts were not fully settled until November 1974, over 24 years after the death of the 10th Duke.

In October 1980, a traveling "Treasures of Chatsworth" exhibition opened at the Royal Academy; and, as such exhibits about the great houses traveled about the world, they proved spectacularly successful at drawing tourists and popular support for country house preservation. By 1998 over five million visitors had come to Chatsworth and the estate was on a secure financial footing. Chatsworth estate still covers about 35,000 acres in Derbyshire and Staffordshire, and employs 66 full-time workers and nearly 100 seasonal workers – among whom are included "a silver steward and a man who winds the clocks."

At the same time that the Devonshires were undertaking their herculean efforts to save their estates, Deborah – as a Mitford – had difficult demands upon her to maintain family ties among her siblings. She was the only Mitford who remained "on speakers" with all of her sisters as they quarreled over family property, old grudges, and the burgeoning literary industry based upon biographies of the family. She was the only sister who ventured to visit Jessica in California; she visited often with Diana and Nancy in France and when they were in England. She was the sister who cleared Pamela's house upon her death. In 2010 Deborah published a memoir, *Wait for Me,* as her one major attempt at the family business of autobiography. Her record of the family life was gentler and more nostalgic than those of her sisters. It was a measure of her family attachment that she took great care in designing and decorating a Devonshire Arms café in Swinbrook. A stopping point for Mitford pilgrims traveling to the churchyard nearby that contains the remains of her famous sisters Nancy, Pamela, Diana, and Unity, the café is decorated with large images of the Mitford siblings.

In addition to her efforts to save the Devonshire properties, maintain detente among her sisters, and raise her own three children; Deborah was a considerable force in maintaining the upper-class social sphere of which, as Duchess of Devonshire, she was the center. Her role and aristocratic presence in English social life was surpassed only by that of the royal family with whom she was friends. Dressed in elegant ermine and tiara, she attended the coronation of Elizabeth II in 1953; she enjoyed dinners and outings with "Cake" – the Queen Mother – and with Charles, the Prince of Wales, whom she referred to as "Friend." Other royal visitors to Chatsworth included the Shah of Persia and the President of India. The Devonshire kinship to the Kennedys meant that the Devonshires attended John Kennedy's inaugural celebrations, visited in the White House (in fact, were present during the Cuban Missile crisis), and were included in President Kennedy's funeral observances.

Having struggled their way back from the brink of economic disaster, the Devonshires were positioned to rekindle the ancient extravagances of their class. In 1965 when their son, Peregrine, came of age, in his honor they held "three lavish parties at Chatsworth: for royalty, for other grandees and gentry, then for the tenantry." In August 1990 when their grandson, Lord Burlington, came of age, the Devonshires had three days of celebrations with 2,400 for a garden party; a small village of tents for a night of dancing, dinner, fireworks; and a third day with charity events with over forty vendors whose charities the Devonshires patronized.

In an accommodation to the changed times, the grand parties of the 11th Duke and Duchess of Devonshire often included people outside of the traditional elite class. When they celebrated their Golden Anniversary in 1991, Andrew and Deborah invited all Derbyshire couples married in 1941 to join them: the marquee covering these diners at Chatsworth was almost a quarter of a mile long. In 1994, for the tercentenary of the Dukedom, nearly 6,000 people attended a riverside pageant that collected money for charity. In July 2000, to mark their fiftieth year as Duke and Duchess and their 80th birthdays, the Devonshires had a fancy-dress party under a large tent on the South Lawn. On this occasion, Deborah "wore the dress made by Worth for Louise, wife of the 9th Duke of Devonshire, for the famous Devonshire House Ball of 1897."

Andrew became a member of his Uncle Harold Macmillan's government (1960-64) as Parliamentary Under-Secretary of State in the Commonwealth Relations Office. Many of his duties were ceremonial and social, as in attending the independence ceremonies in Kenya and Jamaica. A measure of Andrew's playfulness was that on one occasion he "offered 10 pounds to whoever of our party was the first to dance with [the unpopular VP Lyndon Johnson]. Without hesitation Antonia Fraser… cut in, was whirled round the floor and claimed the reward."

Andrew received England's highest honorary rank, that of Knight of the Garter. Deborah received the DCVO (Royal Victorian Order) and other awards for her service to Queen Elizabeth II and to the country. Andrew died May 3, 2004, at age 84; Deborah died on September 24, 2014, at age 94. She is buried with her husband at St. Peter's Church at Edensor on the Chatsworth estate.

CHAPTER 17

LOSS AND RECOVERY: THE FALL OF THE GREAT HOUSES

The case of the Devonshires was among the most successful instances of a family with resources and savvy enough to maintain ownership of its great country estates. Such was not the case for most country houses.

During the World Wars many of these family seats were requisitioned by the government for hospitals, military, or administrative purposes and were often handed back in terrible states of repair. The subsequent maintenance costs were unsustainable; adequate staffing was unaffordable when it could be had at all; and a tax system calculated to pay for England's recent wars, of necessity, had to fall heavily on the elite class that had the only financial wherewithal remaining in the country. In truth, the government was bankrupt, and there seemed only one way to recover financial strength. Inheritance taxes became more aggressive, rising to 65 percent in 1940. Later the debt rose even further when Prime Minister Clement Atlee sought to balance the books for the working class and deliver a National Health Service for all, free at point of service. As noted previously, by the time of Edward Cavendish's death in 1950, inheritance taxes had risen to 80 percent of the total value of the estate. The sole possible relief regarding the "death duties" was that they would be avoided for one generation if the owner were killed during the war.

The costs of preservation and taxes were virtually endless, and aristocrats sought any means for preserving their ancestral homes. Just prior to World War II, the Duke of Newcastle had sold the Hope diamond in an effort to save Clumber Park; but the effort proved insufficient, and his ducal seat was torn down in 1938. Great peers essentially looted their buildings of art treasures, furniture, and portable goods of value to sell in England's weakened postwar art market. In 1959, the Westministers sold £740,000 in artwork. Others sold silver dinner services, furniture, and staircases. Practical re-purposing into schools, colleges, or other enterprises saved many great houses such as St. Donat's. Hearst's castle in Wales is now the United World College of the Atlantic, a boarding school for teenagers with a goal of bringing international understanding among young people. Stowe House escaped demolition by being transformed into a school. The Coal Board bought Himely Hall. Lord Montague turned Beaulieu into a motoring museum. Baliffscourt, built for the Honorable Walter Guinness (later Lord Moyne) in 1931-3, survived as a hotel.

Any method for keeping ownership of the great houses within the family eventually involved opening the estate to public view. Longleat opened for public tours after World War II and in 1966 opened Britain's first safari park on the estate. Estates such as Kedelston Hall and Knebworth House became venues for music festivals. Luton Hoo and Hartwell House became luxury country house hotels, film sets, or venues for events and weddings.

Many such houses simply did not survive. Clause 17 of the Town and Country Planning Act of 1932 sought to prevent demolition of the great houses but was, ironically, opposed by lords such as the Marquess of Hartington (later the Duke of Devonshire) as a restriction upon the lords' ability to do with their estates what they would. Those lords did not foresee that demolition would no longer be a choice but a necessity. Utterly unable to maintain the facilities, the aristocrats had to salvage whatever they could and abandon their homes: "Between 1945 and 1955, four hundred country houses were demolished... Indeed, by 1955, the peak year, they were disappearing at the rate of one every five days." Derwent Hall and the village surrounding it were flooded in order to make a reservoir; the foundations now lie at the bottom of a lake. Streatlem Castle was used for target practice by the Territorial Army. Whitley Park, an estate dating to the Norman Conquest, had its contents sold off, suffered a fire, and was demolished. Aston Clinton was torn down to build a vocational training center. Thorington Hall was pulled down as well.

The Duke of Northumberland demolished Stanwick Park in order to preserve enough assets to save his Alnwick Castle. The rotunda of Nutall Temple was dynamited to make way for the M1 motorway. In 1954 the destruction of Tong Castle was billed as an event open to public viewing as an entertainment. In 1956 Lord Lansdowne demolished a large portion of his great house Bowood. Despite familial ties or architectural significance, nearly 2,000 great houses were demolished. They are now known as "The Lost Houses."

Britain's debates over the survival of these houses eventually took two perspectives. On one hand, it was argued that "in the austere and egalitarian world of Welfare State socialism that followed" World War II, England could not justify subsidizing wealthy people preserving their privileged houses and art at a time when necessities such as food and clothing were still rationed. It grated on the sensibilities of the general public that, at a time when Britons suffered debt, rationing, and their own rebuilding challenges, the wealthy still seemed above the fray. In Britain, clothing was strictly rationed until 1949. Who could feel sympathetic for an aristocrat like Nancy Mitford, who, blithely ensconced in Paris, maintained that dressing well was necessary for one's health? In 1951 Carlos de Bestegui gave a lavish ball in Venice with an exclusive international guest list including Christian Dior, Salvador Dali, Aga Khan III, Pierre Cardin, Nina Ricci; and, among the English attendees were Duff and Diana Manners Cooper, Daisey Fellowes, Cecil Beaton, and Deborah Mitford Cavendish. After the deprivations of two great wars, few ordinary citizens felt the interest in, or saw any need to save, the great country houses that now dotted the land like piles of stone, stone that could be used more profitably in rebuilding homes or barns or anything with a real and immediate usefulness.

The rise of professional politicians further weakened the political power of aristocrats to argue for subsidies or tax relief. Churchill's 1945 cabinet had included six aristocrats among the sixteen members; Macmillan's 1957 cabinet included only four aristocrats out of eighteen members. The House of Lords had no veto power – they could only delay measures – and had no real power beyond strong recommendation. They could not force the government to underwrite preservation of their personal estates. Further, by 1956, "only one-third of the peerage possessed country estates at all." The aristocrats were no longer a ruling or a landed class.

Two of the major preservationist organizations, The National Trust and English Heritage, purchased great houses to preserve them or accepted ownership in exchange for satisfying tax bills and for allowing life residence to the owner. The National Trust for Places of Historic Interest or Natural Beauty was founded in 1898 and has come to own over three hundred nationally important houses that it has restored and opened to the public. In the ten years "between 1947 and 1957 the [government] Treasury passed on twenty-six properties" to the organization's care. English Heritage is a similar organization and is also part of what is sometimes called "the heritage industry." Both organizations have saved significant architecture and art from destruction or dispersion to foreign countries. Properties range in size from Kedelston Hall, Knole, and gardens at Stowe to the homes of famous writers: Kipling's house Bateman's, Virginia Woolf's Monk's House, and Thomas Hardy's Max Gate.

Interestingly, in recent years these preservation groups have come under attack for preserving the houses as museums rather than as working houses. In light of such critiques, both organizations have adjusted their missions to actively farm the estates and provide more vibrant presentations of what William Randolph Hearst valued in 1925 as a truly authentic re-imagining of the past.

The second view regarding preservation of country houses argued that these buildings must be preserved as important examples of the nation's heritage, that their loss would be irreparable. This perspective had a long history of its own. In 1877 William Morris established a Society for the Protection of Ancient Buildings. *Country Life* magazine (established 1897) was published with an eye towards popularizing a "romantic view" of great country houses and the lifestyles of those aristocrats who inhabited them. Ironically, the magazine also later functioned as a compelling market place for the sale of estates. By 1913 an Ancient Monuments Consolidation and Amendment Act was passed to preserve ancient monuments deemed worthy of preservation.

The economic foundations and social philosophy that made these houses possible had disappeared, and so aristocrats sought to make the case for architectural survival on the basis of cultural significance. In this view, the upper class changed their self-concept to view themselves as custodians and curators of their great houses and art collections: "guardians of . . . the national heritage." Perhaps the event that proved pivotal in shifting popular sentiment towards preservation of the great houses was a 1974 exhibition at the Victorian and Albert Museum entitled *The Destruction of the Country House*. The exhibit provided the first widely publicized case for saving the architectural and artistic treasures of the great houses, a case made more persuasive because the public was – often for the first time – allowed to see some of the treasures of these estates. The public and government were persuaded by this argument for national heritage; subsequently "over 370,000 buildings are listed [protected], which includes all buildings erected before 1700 and most constructed before 1840."

Like Deborah Mitford Cavendish's Chatsworth, the Churchillian estate Blenheim Palace would become a success story among the great houses of Britain. Except for closing during a threat from Suffragettes, the grounds and often the palace itself were opened to the public for an entry fee. During World War I it survived as a hospital; during World War II, it escaped bombing and was preserved by housing a college that moved from London to escape the Blitz. In 1950 the palace and grounds were reopened to the public and by 1956 had received their one millionth visitor. The estate offers a maze, adventure playground, mini-train, gift shops, fishing and dining opportunities, and bottled Blenheim mineral water. In recent years the estate raised its profile and earned lucrative contracts by allowing the filming of various internationally successful movies ranging from *The Scarlet Pimpernel* (Anthony Andrews, 1982) to *Harry Potter and the Order of the Phoenix* (Daniel Radcliffe, Emma Watson, Rupert Grint, 2007), *The Young Victoria* (Emily Blunt, Rupert Friend, 2008), *Cinderella* (Lily James, Cate Blanchett, 2015), and *Spectre* (007; Daniel Craig, 2015). The cost in 2009 to repair the "Capability Brown" Dam was £1.8 million. Each year the Marlborough estate must locate finances through tourist dollars or other financial uses in order to maintain the structure and grounds. Still, whispers of the past have not been silenced. On each anniversary of the Battle of Blenheim, the current owner – now the 12th Duke of Marlborough – is required to offer Queen Elizabeth II a copy of the French royal flag as rent for the land on which his palace stands.

EPILOGUE

"It is sometimes not easy having this name"

In 2010, when the British Government proposed to remove all hereditary peers from the House of Lords and make it an entirely elected senate, *The Telegraph* quoted the Dowager Duchess of Devonshire (Deborah Mitford Cavendish): "Titles are meaningless because peers are no longer legislators." Her son the 12th Duke of Devonshire, Peregrine "Stoker" Cavendish claimed that the aristocracy was "dead." At one point he said he considered "dropping the public use of my title."

To date the 12th Duke has not dropped his title and the whiff of aristocratic petulance has subsided. The family home Chatsworth has a chic presence on social media and promotes itself vigorously as a tourist destination, art mecca, and venue for movie-filming and social events. Annually, thousands of Americans flock to see it. Deborah Mitford Cavendish's granddaughter Stella Tennant, who made her career modelling for McQueen and Chanel, has had photo shoots there. The 12th Duke's son William Cavendish—the Earl of Burlington—will inherit the title, multimillion-dollar art collection, and estates. William and his wife Laura, a former model and editor at Harper's Bazaar, are currently doing their apprentice management with the Devonshire's Lismore Castle and have brought edgy contemporary art to this Irish venue. When asked how she will cope with the demands of running a multi-million-dollar estate such as Chatsworth, Laura expressed few concerns: "I'm not planning the curtains or anything."

A new staple in glossy magazines and the tabloid press are photographs of the "Glosse Posse." These are the new generation aristocrats with professional jobs who have developed genuine friendships with the young Royals because they attended the same schools, vacationed together, share an elite social class, and well know the scrutiny of public media. Perhaps the wealthiest of this social set is Hugh Grosvenor who reportedly threw himself a £5 million 21st birthday party. A friend of Prince William, in 2013 he became godfather to Prince George, the future King of England; and in 2016, at age 25, he became the 7th Duke of Westminster with the task of managing a fortune of $13.32 billion. His wealth, passed down through an award of land made in 1677, consists of 300 acres now underlying the expensive and toney Belgravia and Mayfair sections of London.

Another in the group, Harry Soames—grandson of Mary Churchill – attended Ludgrove School with Prince William and Prince Harry. Prince Charles was best man at his parents' wedding. Soames's mother Catherine was a good friend of the princes' mother, Diana, and the families went on ski trips together. He would naturally draw media attention because his father, Sir Nicholas Soames, is a Member of Parliament. However, the name *Churchill* works mightily for and against the young people who bear it. The name meant that Harry Soames's 2014 drunk driving violation was spread across national media. His half-sister Isabella's (impressive) high school report card was posted on the National Churchill Museum website (August 30, 2013). Even Randolph Churchill's 14-year-old granddaughter—Jessica Churchill-McLeod – gained attention for her involvement in a protest march opposing military action against Iraq. Whether desired or not, Churchill descendants always have the attention of the media.

Some had learned to use their name to achieve their own goals. Randolph Churchill's daughter Arabella Spencer-Churchill parleyed her name to gain funding for the Children's World Charity and for the Glastonbury Music Festival. Despite her good works, upon her death in 2007 few of her obituaries avoided noting that she died on the same day that her son Nicholas Barton was sentenced in Australia for his part in a $15 million drug supply operation. In 2018, Diana Churchill's grandson Alex Perkins, who served two tours of duty in Afghanistan, used his name to direct attention to his goal of gaining UK citizenship for Afghan interpreters who are no longer safe in their own country after working with British forces. In press coverage, the 32-year-old was consistently identified as the great-grandson of Churchill who served in the military in Afghanistan and India a century earlier.

Other generations have focused on keeping the eternal flame of Winston Churchill's legacy. Winston's great grandson Randolph, an investment banker, spoke at the 50th anniversary commemoration of Churchill's state funeral, has given Churchill talks at the Royal Albert Hall on "VE Day at 70," and has traveled to give Churchill talks in America with his sister Jennie. Jonathan Sandys, Diana Churchill's grandson, has made it his second career "to continue to teach the lessons of his [Churchill's] legacy," giving 50 speeches per year, maintaining the leadlikechurchill.org website and blog, all while keeping his job as a furniture salesman in Houston, Texas. Movies such as *Darkest Hour* have sent reporters to Sandys for his assessment of which actor has best portrayed his great-grandfather. (His preference was for the late Albert Finney in 2002's *The Gathering Storm*.) Jonathan's brother Duncan Sandys has traveled extensively in the United States and Canada discussing Churchill's talent with painting. Of his 500 paintings, Winston Churchill had time for only one painting during World War II, which he did during the Casablanca Conference with Franklin Roosevelt in 1943. This painting of Marrakesh is now owned by actor Brad Pitt.

The Mitford descendants have shared similar degrees of national exposure because of their Mitford connections. On one hand, Diana Mitford's great-granddaughter supermodel Jasmine Guinness told one interviewer, "It's great to know where your roots lie and where everything truly began, because that goes to the heart of your identity. We are here, and that in itself is an achievement of our ancestors." Diana Mitford's granddaughter Daphne Guinness has traded on her family wealth and name to become a fashion icon: famously, she owns 2,500 garments, 450 pairs of shoes, and 200 handbags. She has dabbled in filmmaking and has released two albums, *Optimist in Black* (2016) and *Daphne & The Golden Chord* (1018). Despite her boldness and the endless financial resources provided by the Guinness fortune when she was growing up, Daphne felt blackballed at school if she mentioned that Oswald and Diana Mosley were her grandparents. When his Diana died in 2003, both Jonathan Guinness (3rd Lord Moyne) and daughter Daphne wrote letters to *The Daily Telegraph* protesting the obituary written by Andrew Roberts on August 13, 2003, that seemed to malign Diana's reputation.

In particular, Diana's children by Oswald Mosley have shunned public attention. Her eldest son by Mosley, Oswald Alexander, spent his life in France out of the public eye, though his wife Charlotte continued the family publication legacy by editing the Mitford family letters. Alexander's younger brother Max found a career in the 1960s away from politics in the budding Formula One racing world. However, in March 2008, newspapers exposed a Nazi-themed sadomasochistic sex session with prostitutes in a Chelsea apartment. Mosley sued the newspaper for breach of privacy, and won; but the legacy of his famous fascist parents stayed with him. When his brilliant 39-year-old publicity-shy son Alexander died the next year from a suspected heroin overdose, a cousin would tell *The Telegraph*, "It is sometimes not easy having this name."

Jessica Mitford's daughter Constancia "Dinky" Romilly had two children by the American Civil Rights leader James Forman. Constancia's son, James Forman Jr., is a professor of law at Yale. Son Chaka has pursued a career in television and movies. Jessica's son Ben Treuhaft has been unconventional in continuing his grandmother's protest against the customs of society. In the 1990s he used his trade as piano tuner to be politically active, particularly in flouting the Cuba embargo by sending pianos to Cuba. In 2014, he challenged the city council of Edinburgh, Scotland, by setting up his piano and a tent on the city beach and proposing to live there.

Americans travel to Britain precisely because of the royal and aristocratic vestiges that remain there. Americans flock to tour the great houses and attend events such as the Chelsea flower show. Americans now build and sail yachts in the Cowes yacht races. American television now covers horse racing at Royal Ascot. Shooting in Scotland is still favored in August. Public schools still retain an aristocratic sensibility. Ancient names remain and titles still strike a frisson in social gatherings even though their traditional power and influence is diminished. Although most aristocrats must now follow conventional pathways to power on the boards of technology companies, international corporations, and banks, the architectural history of their great houses, such as Blenheim Castle and Chatsworth, continue to awe and engage. The world in which the 10th Duke of Marlborough was bewildered that a toothbrush "wasn't foaming"—because his valet had always prepared it for him—was a world of appalling privilege from which we can scarcely take our eyes.

Why does the English aristocracy continue to intrigue Americans? We tell ourselves that we dusted our feet of them with the American Revolution, creating a country that has been entirely independent in politics and the arts— if we can bring ourselves to overlook two World Wars. Or if we can overlook the immense interlayering of our countries: our Emily Dickinson with their Jane Austen; our Sam Spade with their Sherlock Holmes; our Beach Boys with their Beatles; our Ronald Reagan with their Margaret Thatcher.

The truth is that the child never truly divorces a parent country. We are interested in the English upper class because they have given us reason to be so. Their houses, their manners, and the powerful ways in which they shaped the twentieth century—and our contemporary society—will resist our forgetting them and our efforts to consign them to the historical dustbin of irrelevant matters.

ACKNOWLEDGEMENTS

Thanks to Justin Hobson, Manager of the Picture Library at *Country Life,* for his kind help in locating and providing me with the 1921 St. Donat's article.

I am grateful to Hannah Dakin, Lauren Bailey, Joe Shillito, and the Matador publishing staff for their impressive responsiveness and help in the publication of this manuscript.

No writer can survive without good readers and excellent feedback. Mac Griswold helpfully critiqued my chapter summaries. Cathy Cochran, Laura Farley, Sara Reed, and Sally Southall were early readers and encouragers. Alicia Kanny Nevins gave the first thorough editing of my manuscript and was unfailingly accurate in her advice. Eileen Ford and Liz Addison were sturdy workhorses in editing multiple drafts, offering guidance on revisions, and bolstering whenever confidence faltered. I cannot thank them enough.

NOTES

Chapter 1

1   "I get tired of going up there and camping": Mark Wilson (forward by Lynn Forney McMurray), *Julia Morgan: Architect of Beauty*, (Utah: Gibbs Smith, 2007), 5.

2   Western Union Telegram: Clive Aslet, *The Last Country Houses*, (New Haven and London: Yale University Press, 1982), 198.

3   He wrote approvingly about St. Donat's varied specimens: F. H. Cripps-Day, "The St. Donat's Castle Armoury," (*Country Life*, 2 April 1921), 415.

4   A hundred men worked on the Welsh project Hearst finished refurbishing: Aslet, *Country Houses*, 211.

5   And so, much of the décor added to the house was native to Britain: Aslet, Country Houses, 207.

6   Claridges and the Savoy supplied chefs: St. Donats, stradling.org.uk.

7   George Bernard Shaw was to have said: Nathan Bevan, "Lydia Hearst is Queen of the Castle," Wales Online https://www.walesonline.co.uk/news/wales-news/lydia-hearst-queen-castle-2156003, 2 August 2008. Accessed June 10, 2019.

8   "The rich 'are different from you and me'": F. Scott Fitzgerald, "The Rich Boy," (*Redbook* 1926).

Chapter 2

9   Lady Churchill lay "sprawled on their] velvet capes and feather boas": William Manchester, *The Last Lion: Winston Spencer Churchill, Visions of Glory, 1874-1932,* (New York: Little, Brown and Company, 1983), 107.

10   This ducal seat: Gail MacColl and Carol McD. Wallace, *To Marry an English Lord: Tales of Wealth and Marriage, Sex and Snobbery,* (New York: Workman Publishing Company, Inc., 1989, 2012), 218.

11   The poet Alexander Pope wrote of her: Ralph G. Martin, *Jennie: The Life of Lady*

Randolph Churchill, 1854-1895, (Englewood Cliffs, N. J.: Prentice-Hall, Inc., 1969), 62.

12   Here Sarah boldly called in all of her social capital: Martin, *Jennie*, 61.

13   A later royal ruler, King George III: Martin, *Jennie*, 61.

14   Not satisfied with that unimpeded view afforded by the ha-ha: Bill Bryson, *At Home: A Short History of Private Life* (New York: Anchor Books, 2010), 307.

15   The Carnarvon family hired the landscape darling: Bryson, *At Home*, 310.

16   In the 1880s — just prior to Winston Churchill's birth: Barbara Tuchman, *The Proud Tower: A Portrait of The World Before the War, 1890-1914*, (New York: The Library of America, 1962, 2012), 595.

17   Even a relatively minor peer, George Herbert, the 5th Earl of Carnarvon: The Countess of Carnarvon, *Lady Almina and The Real Downton Abbey: The Lost Legacy of Highclere Castle*, (New York: Broadway Paperbacks, 2011), 2.

18   But the 2nd Duke of Sutherland trumped all other peers: David Cannadine, *The Decline and Fall of the British Aristocracy*, (New York: Vintage Books, 1999), Appendix A, 710-711.

19   Not surprisingly, in 1880 the land in London owned by the 1st Duke of Westminster: Cannadine, *The Decline*, Appendix A, 710. Currency conversion: https://www.measuringworth.com/calculators/exchange/result_exchange.php

20   The vast estates and labor force could take full advantage: Philip Steele, *Encyclopedia of British History*, (Great Bardfield, Essex: Miles Kelly Publishing Ltd, 2001), 163.

21   "'They [The English lords] had learned the practice of government'": Tuchman, *The Proud Tower*, 568.

22   At their zenith in Balfour's Cabinet: Cannadine, *The Decline,* Appendix B, 711.

Chapter 3

23   There was no doubt that William Vanderbilt paid the Duke a dowry: Catherine Bailey, *The Secret Rooms: A True Story of A Haunted Castle, A Plotting Duchess, & A Family Secret,* (New York: Penguin Books, 2012), 2012 conversion, 184.

24   Consuelo Vanderbilt's case was dramatic: Bryson, *At Home, 258.*

25   There also was "constant pressure not to do 'The Wrong Thing'": The Countess of Carnarvon, *Lady Almina,* 74.

26   "'It is quite as vulgar to hang back'": The Countess of Carnarvon, *Lady Almina,* 74.

27   In London, aristocrats at their exclusive clubs on Pall Mall: Tuchman, *The Proud Tower,* 584.

28   For example, in 1895 the Secretary of War, Lord Lansdowne: Tuchman, *The Proud Tower,* 587.

29   In fact, Mitford is listed as one of the possible fathers: Lovell, *The Sisters: The Saga of the Mitford Family* (New York: W. W. Norton & Company, Inc., 2001), 14.

30   David survived a leg wound: Lovell, *The Sisters,* 14.

31   Sydney, though sobered by home responsibilities: Lovell, *The Sisters,* 13.

Chapter 4

32   Winston was born in a time of "imperial heroes": Manchester, *Lion,* 43.

33   Then, like other wealthy young men, he followed his graduation with the Grand Tour": Martin, *Jennie,* 57.

34   The Duke wrote to Randolph, "Never was there such an illustration of the adage'": Martin, *Jennie,* 65.

35   Jenny's father, Leonard Jerome, was acceptably wealthy: Manchester, *Lion,* 104.

36   Leonard, hearing of the Duke's opposition, cable Mrs. Jerome, "'CONSENT WITHDRAWN'": Martin, *Jennie,* 71.

37   Jennie was probably pregnant: Manchester, *Lion,* 104.

38   Although the *London Times* officially noted: Manchester, *Lion,* 108.

39   Hartington burned the letters: Manchester, *Lion,* 114.

40   The affair itself ended: Manchester, *Lion,* 115.

41   "'I could never make out what those damned dots'": Manchester, *Lion,* 147.

42   Historians still debate whether the cause of death: Manchester, *Lion,* 97; Churchill Centre and Museum.

Chapter 5

43   The Devonshire invitation had encouraged guests" MacColl, *To Marry,* 282.

44   Fanny Ronalds, representing Euterpe: MacColl, *To Marry,* 282.

45   The Prince of Wales was grand: Cannadine, *The Decline,* 343.

46   When Manchester finally died: MacColl, *To Marry,* 252.

47   "'Everywhere one met friends'": Virginia Cowles, *Winston Churchill: The Era and the Man,* (New York: Harper & Brothers Publishers, 1953), 42.

48   The cost of a debut: Sally Bedell Smith, *Reflected Glory: The Life of Pamela Churchill Harriman,* (New York: Simon & Schuster, 1996), 35.

49   A wardrobe for The Season: MacColl, *To Marry,* 71.

50   If a lady wore "a crescent instead of a tiara": Aslet, *Country Houses,* 17.

51   The best place to learn how to curtsey: Caroline Taggart, *Her Ladyship's Guide To the British Season,* (London: National Trust Books, 2013), 35.

52   Dress for the evening was strictly prescribed: Taggart, *Guide,* 26.

53   Families such as the Devonshires could use their town home: Smith, *Reflected Glory,* 52.

54   In 1939 the Duke and Duchess of Marlborough gave a ball: Smith, *Reflected Glory,* 52.

55   By the twentieth century a definite pattern had coalesced: Smith, *Reflected Glory,* 42.

56   One former debutante, Angela Lambert, remarked: Smith, *Reflected Glory,* 40.

57   Sarah Churchill recalled that a maid kept a register: Sarah Churchill, *Sarah*

Churchill: Keep on Dancing, (New York: Coward, McCann & Geoghegan, 1981), 36.

58   "'Family was essential'": Smith, *Reflected Glory*, 9, 12.

59   One observer wrote, "it seemed as if 'a race of gods gods and goddesses'": Tuchman, *Proud Tower*, 582.

60   In 1911, the *Tatler* magazine reported": Sarah Warwick, *Upstairs and Downstairs*, (London: Carlton Publishing Group, 2011), 2016 conversion, 82.

61   The speed with which servants could re-load guns: Aslet, *Country Houses*, 71.

62   The elite then dispersed: Taggart, *Guide*, 13, 17.

63   And, despite the "antiquated twelve-mile-an-hour speed limit": Aslet, *Country Houses*, 51.

64   "'Saturday to Monday'": Warwick, *Upstairs*, 60.

65   Ladies could have twenty-five changes of clothing: Aslet, *Country Houses*, 58.

66   A competent hostess insured: MacColl, *To Marry*, 294.

67   Because each guest had a servant: Tuchman, *Proud Tower*, 595.

68   As one debutante later explained: Smith, *Reflected Glory*, 44.

69   Personal maids or the "upstairs servants": Smith, *Reflected Glory*, 45.

70   The country house party offered men the opportunity to hunt: Aslet, *Country Houses*, 8.

71   An invitation from a titled host: Aslet, *Country Houses*, 19.

72   The Duke of Rutland's "family could always tell by the speed of morning prayers": Tuchman, *Proud Tower*, 591.

73   On the final day of her life: Tuchman, *Proud Tower*, 571.

74   One famously-repeated anecdote from the 1890s: Bryson, *At Home*, 106.

75   To avoid such confusions, guests at Wentworth Woodhouse: Bryson, *At Home*, 106.

76   Another device was to have a bell "rung at 6 a.m. to warn": Warwick, *Upstairs*, 115.

77   Within this world was a physical division: Warwick, *Upstairs*, 7.

78   At the end of a visit: Warwick, *Upstairs*, 60.

Chapter 6

79   "'More of the panther than of the woman in her look'": Martin, *Jennie*, 126.

80   One of his lovers was the world renown singer Jenny Lind: Martin, *Jennie*, 1.

81   The next year at Cowes Jennie met the twenty-three-year-old Randolph Churchill: Martin, *Jennie*, 49.

82   "Only the legitimacy of the first patrician child counted": Manchester, *Lion*, 88.

83   "Never remarking on the paternal resemblance": Lisa Hilton, Lisa, *The Horror of Love: Nancy Mitford and Gaston Palewski in Paris and London*, (New York and London: Pegasus Books, 2011), 204.

84   It was said, "'He was the kind of man'": Martin, *Jennie*, 134.

85   Winston didn't even know: Manchester, *Lion*, 149.

86   What little contact Randolph had with Winston: Manchester, *Lion*, 182-183.

87   Winston desperately sought the approval of his mother: Manchester, *Lion*, 172.

88   While Winston was a student at Harrow: Martin, *Jennie*, 256.

89   Winston wrote his mother, "'You must stick up for me'": Martin, *Jennie*, 257.

90   Even though he was just a young boy: Martin, *Jennie*, 313.

91   While he recuperated from a ruptured spleen: Martin, *Jennie*, 310-311.

92   On a third attempt, Winston did pass the entrance exam for Sandhurst: Martin, *Jennie*, 313.

93   The case was settled for about $70,000: Martin, *Jennie*, 46-50.

94   Jennie ultimately had nearly twenty lovers: Martin, *Jennie*, 137.

95   According to a *New York Times* headline, "'British Society [Was] Astonished'": MacColl, *To Marry*, 273.

96   In 1918 at age 64 she married Montague Porch: MacColl, *To Marry*, 337.

97   Amid the panic and moans: Manchester, *Lion*, 643.

98   Winston's personal secretary, Eddie Marsh: Mary Soames, *Clementine Churchill: The Biography of a Marriage*, (New York: Paragon House Publishers, 1979), 68-69.

99   After a few days, gangrene set in: Manchester, *Lion*, 759.

Chapter 7

100   Second Lieutenant Winston Churchill wrote Jennie Jerome Churchill: Ralph G. Martin, *Jennie: The Life of Lady Randolph Churchill, The Dramatic Years, 1895-1921,* (New York: Prentice Hall Press, 1971*)*, 63.

101   Jennie replied as though agreeing to a boyish lark: Manchester, *Lion*, 223.

102   Sometimes they lead military charges: Manchester, *Lion*, 222.

103   As early as 1817 John Wilson had proudly declared: Manchester, *Lion*, 44.

104   The genuine pride in the world-embracing influence of the Empire: Manchester, *Lion*, 45.

105   Days consisted of 90 minutes of drills: Cowles, *Churchill*, 45.

106   Under his terms of duty: Cowles, *Churchill*, 43.

107   Churchill was ecstatic: Manchester, *Lion*, 251.

108   On the other hand: Manchester, *Lion*, 260.

109   In 1898 he called on several social connections: Boris Johnson, *The Churchill Factor: How One Man Made History*, (New York: Riverhead Books, 2014), 61.

110   The time frame was so immediate: Tuchman, *Proud Tower*, 588.

111   At one point Kitchener kept repeating: William Wright, *Omdurman 1898: Battle Story* (Gloucestershire, U. K.: Spellmount, 2012), 209.

112   Churchill himself participated in perhaps the last successful cavalry charge: Manchester, *Lion*, 280.

113   To many imperialists like Cecil Rhodes: Piers Brendon, *The Decline and Fall of the British Empire, 1781-1997*, (New York: Alfred A. Knopf, 2008), 194.

114   Churchill, now captured: Manchester, *Lion*, 301.

115   He wrote his mother: Manchester, *Lion*, 304.

116 After days of struggle and wandering: Manchester, *Lion*, 308.

117 When he finally passed into safe Portuguese East Africa: Manchester, *Lion*, 314.

118 We should show: Brendon, *The Decline*, 4.

119 These "Randlords"-a term coined by their currency – returned to England: Aslet, *Country Houses*, 32.

120 As Clive Aslet observed, "country-house building was quite an accurate index": Aslet, *Country Houses*, 34.

121 Shipping and shipbuilding: Aslet, *Country Houses*, 34, 4, 56.

122 He was able to purchase Elveden: Bryson, *At Home*, 105.

123 At his other estate, Hever Castle: Aslet, *Country Houses*, 302-303.

124 Wags would suggest: Aslet, *Country Houses*, 194.

125 In speaking to the Architectural Association: Anna Pavord, *Hidcote Manor Garden*, (Swindon, Wiltshire: National Trust Enterprises Ltd., 2004), 7-8.

126 Architect Edwin Lutyens not only designed: Aslet, *Country Houses*, 42.

127 Country houses were built by one of two types of owner: Aslet, *Country Houses*, 7.

128 In his excellent study *The Last Country Houses*: Aslet, *Country Houses*, 3.

Chapter 8

129 "'Was this the face that launched a thousand ships?'": Bailey, *Secret Rooms*, 297.

130 Violet Asquith, the Prime Minister's daughter: Manchester, *Lion*, 394.

131 In 1904 when Clementine was first introduced: Manchester, *Lion*, 394.

132 Her sister Nellie suggested: Soames, *Clementine*, 37.

133 Blanche herself told Lady Londonderry that Clementine's father was Blanche's brother-in-law: Mary S. Lovell, *The Churchills: In Love and War*, (New York: W. W. Norton & Company, 2011), 24-25.

134 Clementine dazzled in a gown of white satin: Soames, *Clementine*, 65.

135 In the nine years since his Boer War escape, Churchill had parleyed his fame: Cowles, *Churchill*, 136-137.

136 First, the English agricultural system became depressed: Cannadine, *The Decline*, 56.

137 This broader voting franchise threatened: Cannadine, *The Decline*, 27.

138 Finally, he proposed what the nobles derisively called: Cowles, *Churchill*, 128.

139 Lloyd George contended: Cowles, *Churchill*, 129

140 By any objective assessment: Manchester, *Lion*, 408.

141 Freshly-minted Liberal Winston Churchill: Cowles, *Churchill*, 127.

142 Though by contemporary standards: Cannadine, *The Decline*, 48.

143 Churchill wryly joked that attacking the Dukes: Cowles, *Churchill*, 131.

144 Winston's exasperated ducal cousin "Sunny" Marlborough: Soames, *Clementine*, 127.

145 Turncoat Churchill was widely attacked: Cowles, *Churchill*, 132.

146 How, he asked: Cannadine, *The Decline*, 49.

147 The pressure became so great that Edward secretly agreed: Cannadine, *The Decline*, 52.

148 By 1920, the Duke of Rutland was forced to sell 27,000 acres: Cannadine, *The Decline*, 725-726.

149 Some of the Prince's friends: Aslet, *Country Houses*, 16.

150 In 1870 he became the first Prince of Wales in history: MacColl, *To Marry*, 18.

151 His lovers were numerous: Manchester, *Lion*, 137.

152 In 1899 as Prince Edward, he snubbed the 80-year-old Duke of Richmond: Aslet, *Country Houses*, 19.

153 He instead stayed at nearby Moulton Paddocks: Aslet, *Country Houses*, 28.

154 They attended to his smallest desires: MacColl, *To Marry*, 288.

155 Though his official residence was now Buckingham Palace: MacColl, *To Marry*, 83.

156 "He traveled with two valets": MacColl, *To Marry*, 301.

157 When, as King he visited Kylemore Abbey: MacColl, *To Marry*, 288-289.

158 Alfred was the fabulously wealthy son: The Countess of Carnarvon, *Lady Almina*, 30.

159 With Almina's inheritance the Earl would renovate Highclere Castle and finance his Egyptian explorations that eventually resulted in the discovery of the tomb of King Tutankhamen.

160 For this three-day visit, the Rothschild wealth spent nearly $1.5 million": The Countess of Carnarvon, *Lady Almina*, 46-47.

161 Under Edward's aegis, money: Aslet, *Country Houses*, 16.

162 It was a measure of his wife Alexandra's patience: MacColl, *To Marry*, 251.

Chapter 9

163 On Monday, August 3, 1914, Sir Edward Grey famously remarked: Cannadine, *The Decline*, 72.

164 Kipling complained loudly: Adam Hochschild, *To End All Wars: A Story of Loyalty and Rebellion, 1914-1918*, (Boston: Houghton Mifflin Harcourt, 2011), 70, 69.

165 In 1914 alone 1,186,351 British citizens: Max Hastings, *Catastrophe 1914: Europe Goes To War*, (New York: Alfred A. Knopf, 2013: 521. Willmott, H. P. *World War I*. New York: DK Publishing, 2003), 125.

166 Author H. G. Wells in writing for the *Daily Chronicle* observed: Bailey, *Secret Rooms*, 249.

167 Wells's collected newspaper article: Ian Westwell, *The Complete Illustrated History of World War I*. (Wigston: Leicestershire Hermes House: 2011), 251.

168 When World War I began: Cannadine, *The Decline*, 44.

169 As historian David Cannadine summarized it: Cannadine, *The Decline*, 73-74.

170 Dr. A. A. David, the headmaster of the prestigious boarding school Rugby, wrote: Hastings, *Catastrophe*, 422.

171 An editorial in *The Times Educational Supplement* argued: Hastings, *Catastrophe*, 422.

172 Nellie Hozier, Clementine Churchill's sister, immediately went to Belgium: Soames, *Clementine*, 146.

173 The list of houses was a lengthy one: Simon Greaves, *The Country House at War: Fighting the Great War at Home and in the Trenches,* (London: National Trust Books, 2014), 36.

174 As a measure of the gentlemanly terms: Hastings, *Catastrophe*, 522.

175 Colonel Douglas Haig, veteran of the Boer Wars: Tuchman, *Proud Tower*, 594.

176 Once arrived near Menin in Belgium: Hastings, *Catastrophe*, 476.

177 Generals recruited their personal staffs: Bailey, *Secret Rooms*, 320.

178 Aristocrats still attempted to enjoy many customary luxuries: Bailey, *Secret Rooms*, 321.

179 At the battle of Sharpenburg: Bailey, *Secret Rooms*, 323.

180 At least one officer had "*Country Life* [magazine] sent out to the trenches": Aslet, *Country Houses*, 42.

181 "One Grenadier officer placed an order with Fortnum & Mason": Hastings, *Catastrophe*, 517.

182 The grandson of the Duke of Westminster wrote his mother: Hochschild, *To End All Wars*, xiv.

183 Any assault through the barbed wire of No Man's Land: Manchester, *Lion*, 507.

184 On an average day: Manchester, *Lion*, 508.

185 By 1915 the Germans added the insidious, Countess of Carnarvon, *Lady Almina*, 200-201.

186 At the second Battle of Ypres: Countess of Carnarvon, *Lady Almina*, 156.

187 In the Battle of the Somme: Countess of Carnarvon, *Lady Almina*, 196.

188 The battle of Passchendaele: Countess of Carnarvon, *Lady Almina*, 206.

189 In the first three months of the war: Hastings, *Catastrophe*, 422.

190 Thirty-one percent: Hochschild, *To End All Wars*, xiv.

191 By the end of that first year: Cannadine, *The Decline*, 74.

192 World War I was especially deadly for aristocrats: Hochschild, *To End All Wars*, xiv.

193 By 1917 a fifth of aristocrats: Bailey, *Secret Rooms*, 409.

194 Prime Ministers Herbert Asquith: Hochschild, *To End All Wars*: xiv.

195 Machen, Arthur. *The Bowmen and Other Legends of the War.* Centenary New: The First World War, 1914-1918. https://centenarynews.com/article?id=1679. Accessed May 24, 2919.

196 One German set up a Christmas tree: Hochschild, *To End All Wars*: 130.

197 They collected their dead: Countess of Carnarvon, *Lady Almina*, 149.

198 By Christmas afternoon: Hochschild, *To End All Wars*, 130.

199 One royal effort consisted of sending: Hochschild, *To End All Wars*: 129.

200 He was particularly appalled by the number of British officers slain: Hochschild, *To End All Wars*, 302.

201 Rudyard Kipling, who also lost a son in the war: Hochschild, *To End All Wars*, 303.

202 At the very same time his father, the Duke of Rutland: Bailey, *Secret Rooms*, 232.

203 The combination of inexperienced pilots and unreliable aircraft technology: Steele, *Encyclopedia,* 205.

204 At the beginning of the war: Bailey, *Secret Rooms*, 248.

205 An unprecedented practice of shaming men to enlist: Willmott, *World War I*, 127.

206 The conservative tabulation of World War I deaths: Hochschild, *To End All Wars*, 347-348.

207 Nearly a million military deaths occurred: Hastings, *Catastrophe*, 561.

208 In fact, "…Britain…suffered more casualties in World War I": Westwell, *Illustrated*, 520.

209 Of every 20 British men: Hochschild, *To End All Wars*, 347-348.

210 In Britain, 41,000 survivors had limb amputations: Countess of Carnarvon, *Lady Almina*, 182.

211 Even the United States Congress refused: Westwell, *Illustrated*, 237.

Chapter 10

212 For his part, in 1914 Winston Churchill was ebullient: Brendon, *The Decline*, 228.

213 On September 21, 1914, he affirmed that the Germans were now afraid: Cowles, *Churchill*, 177.

214 He seemed willing to manage all areas of government: Manchester, *Lion*, 481.

215 The Irish were disloyal: Manchester, *Lion*, 456.

216 His marines should attack: Manchester, *Lion*, 499.

217 He advised the army: Cowles, *Churchill*, 180.

218 An official inquiry into the debacle of the Dardanelles: Manchester, *Lion*, 614.

219 November 1922 brought another type of stress to the family: Cowles, *Churchill*, 243.

Chapter 11

220 The Churchills had pet names for all of their children: Manchester, *Lion*, 757.

221 Winston grieved that this little life: Manchester, *Lion*, 758.

222 In the heat of battle: Countess of Carnarvon, *Lady Almina*, 166.

223 Rudyard Kipling, shaken by his son John's death: Hochschild, *To End All Wars*, 363.

224 On November 11, 1920, when King George V unveiled this Cenotaph: Countess of Carnarvon, *Lady Almina*, 239.

225 During the ceremony the entire nation was silent: Hochschild, *To End All Wars*, 348.

226 Literary works like Eric Remarque's: Westwell, *Illustrated*, 251.

227 The war had virtually bankrupted Britain: Manchester, *Lion*, 787.

228 By 1919 lords such as the Earl of Carnarvon: Countess of Carnarvon, *Lady Almina*, 279.

229 The Castle Howard estate: Bryson, *At Home*, 525.

230 George Washington Vanderbilt, Andrew Mellon, Henry Clay Frick: Bryson, *At Home*, 525.

231 In 1925 Thomas C. Williams purchased Agecroft Hall: Bryson, *At Home*, 526.

232 Two years later she gave an engagement ball: Countess of Carnarvon, *Lady Almina*, 244.

233 He found the tomb in 1922: Countess of Carnarvon, *Lady Almina*, 245.

234 The interwar years—the Roaring Twenties: Cannadine, *The Decline*, 352.

235 Diana Manners, the "Helen": Bailey, *Secret Rooms*, 298.

236 The Old Guard seemed to retreat: Cannadine, *The Decline*, 353.

Chapter 12

237 "*Why* did I dedicate the beastly book": Charlotte Mosley, ed. *The Mitfords: Letters Between Six Sisters*, (London: Fourth Estate: 2012), 22.

238 The cheeriest familial response: Charlotte Mosley, *Mitfords*, 22.

239 She believed in class-consciousness: Hilton, *Horror*, 20.

240 When Jessica and Deborah were playing in the churchyard: Lovell, *Sisters*, 45; Devonshire, *Chickens*, 181.

241 She nicknamed her youngest sister: Lovell, *Sisters*, 54.

242 In contradiction to her jaundiced view of her parents: Hilton, *Horror*, 29; Lovell, *Sisters*, 73.

243 She announced she was unofficially engaged to Hamish St Clair-Erskine: Hilton, *Horror*, 34-37.

244 The most life-changing result: Lovell, *Sisters*, 67.

245 The model for Anthony Blanche: Lovell, *Sisters*, 68.

246 Her father found these friends intolerable: Charlotte Mosley, *Mitfords*, xx, 183. Deborah (Mitford) Devonshire, *Counting My Chickens and Other Home Thoughts*, (New York: Farrar, Straus and Giroux, 2001), 181.

247 Her witty column whetted people's interest for gossip: Lovell, *Sisters*, 107.

248 Her parents clearly had idiosyncrasies: Lovell, *Sisters*, 31.

249 Bedroom windows had to be open six inches: Devonshire, *Chickens*, 185.

250 He bought a miniature pony and brought him home in a cab: Lovell, *Sisters*, 27.

251 When collecting the offering at church: Devonshire, *Chickens*, 189.

252 Perhaps unsurprisingly in 1938 he purchased a small Scottish island: Hilton, *Horror*, 88.

253 Farve/Uncle Matthew and his friends: Nancy Mitford, *The Pursuit of Love*, (New York: Vantage Books of Random House, 2010), 11.

254 In a memoir Nancy recorded an incident: Nancy Mitford, *The Water Beetle*, (London: Hamish Hamilton, 1962), 6-9.

255 Their mother endured the public humiliations: Lovell, *Sisters*, 473.

256 Sometime after 1932 she attempted suicide: Hilton, *Horror*, 39.

257 Her rejection by St. Clair-Erskine: Lovell, *Sisters*, 151.

258 Urbanely, Nancy appeared to accept the situation: Lovell, *Sisters*, 213.

259 Her 1935 novel *Wigs on the Green*: Lovell, *Sisters*, 169.

260 The Mitford family sent the Rodds to Spain: Hilton, *Horror*, 79.

261 Although they were unsuccessful with Jessica: Hilton, *Horror*, 86.

262 Pamela, born on November 25, 1907: Lovell, *Sisters*, 30.

263 Pamela did not return the engagement ring: Lovell, *Sisters*, 96-97.

264 Writer John Betjeman fell in love with Pamela: Lovell, *Sisters*, 128-129.

265 By the mid-1930s, though, Pamela had fallen in love again: Lovell, *Sisters*, 214.

266 Derek and Pamela agreed to marry: Lovell, *Sisters*, 215.

267 If Pamela had a noteworthy political moment: Lovell, *Sisters*, 55.

268 She, like her siblings, traveled to Germany: Lovell, *Sisters,* 186.

269 He was sent off to boarding school: Lovell, *Sisters,* 42.

270 While at Eton, according to James-Lees Milne: Lovell, *Sisters*, 93.

271 Several of the men piled into seven small planes: Lovell, *Sisters*, 114-116.

272 Soon he traveled to Germany itself: Lovell, *Sisters*, 93.

273 Even Winston Churchill, when visiting in Italy: Cowles, *Churchill*, 271-272.

274 In family friend James Lee-s Milne's words, "'Divine isn't the word'": Lovell, *Sisters*, 80.

275 As a teenager playing the organ: Devonshire, *Chickens*, 103.

276 The Churchill men accompanied Diana: Lovell, *Sisters*, 83, 79.

277 Before The Season had concluded, she was engaged: Lovell, *Sisters*, 94.

278 A premier social event: Lovell, *Sisters*, 100.

279 But their London house at 10 Buckingham Street: Lovell, *Sisters*, 127, 108. Eerily, it was while at Biddesden that the Guinnesses innocently loaned Bryan's gun to friend and neighbor Dora Carrington, who killed herself after her lover Lytton Strachey's death (Lovell, *Sisters*, 129, 132).

280 A thinly-veiled record of the adventures: Lovell, *Sisters*, 110.

281 However, also in 1930 Bryan and Diana visited Tom: Lovell, *Sisters*, 106-107.

282 Diana's newfound interest in Fascism: Lovell, *Sisters*, 131.

283 Mosley was wealthy, had impeccable social credentials: Lovell, *Sisters*, 139.

284 Winston Churchill himself proposed Mosley for membership in The Other Club: Lovell, *Sisters*, 135.

285 Mosley was also an unrepentant womanizer: Hilton, *Horror*, 205.

286 Diana refused to lie to her husband: Lovell, *Sisters*, 114.

287 The situation roiled even further when Cynthia Mosley: Hilton, *Horror*, 45.

288 Because both Tom and Unity had social connect: Lovell, *Sisters*, 160.

289 Diana eventually visited Germany four times: Lovell, *Sisters*, 208.

290 In fact, after the 1936 Olympics: Lovell, *Sisters*, 205.

291 During one of the 1936 visits to Germany: Lovell, *Sisters*, 221.

292 An innocuous token of her aloofness: Lovell, *Sisters*, 51.

293 Though she achieved Nancy's goal: Lovell, *Sisters*, 120.

294 Unity followed the traditional practice: Lovell, *Sisters*, 124.

295 She stole stationery from Buckingham Palace: Charlotte Mosley, *Mitfords*, 11.

296 Carried a pet rat: Lovell, *Sisters*, 125.

297 The galvanizing political moment: Lovell, *Sisters*, 171.

298 "Such a terribly exciting thing happened yesterday": Charlotte Mosley, *Mitfords*, 46.

299 Having noticed the repeated presence of this young woman: Lovell, *Sisters*, 181.

300 They became such friendly companions: Lovell, *Sisters*, 183-184.

301 American journalist Virginia Cowles: Virginia Cowles, *Looking For Trouble*, (New York and London: Harper & Brothers, 1941): 148.

302 In Cowles's opinion: Cowles, *Looking*, 152.

303 Unity's brother, Tom Mitford, was a friend of mine: Cowles, *Looking*, 148.

304 Hitler accepted Unity's adoration: Cowles, *Looking*, 150, 152-153.

305 At one party Cowles observed: Cowles, *Looking*, 151.

306 Nancy's novel *Wigs on the Green*: Lovell, *Sisters*, 169.

307 She wrote to a German newspaper: Lovell, *Sisters*, 187-188.

308 She became so notorious: Lovell, *Sisters*, 202-203.

309 The British press opined,"'At It Again, the Mad, Mad Mitfords'": Lovell, *Sisters*, 265.

310 Impervious to the criticism: Lovell, *Sisters*, 205.

311 She rode to the 1936 Wagner Festival: Lovell, *Sisters*, 207.

312 In 1937 British newspapers rumored: Lovell, *Sisters*, 246, 280.

313 On one hand, she attended the coronation: Charlotte Mosley, *Mitfords*, 90.

314 Politically naïve, Unity was surprised: Lovell, *Sisters*, 266.

315 She was dazzled by flowers: Lovell, *Sisters*, 267.

316 When Hitler gave her an apartment, she blithely wrote that this perfect apartment belonged to "to a young Jewish couple who are going abroad. Lovell, *Sisters*, 284-285.

317 Thus, it was not surprising that as war between England and Germany loomed: Lovell, *Sisters*, 289.

318 She, too, developed a private language with Unity. The name "Hons" was because of their affection for poultry, not because their rank made them "Honourables." Lovell, *Sisters*, 52.

319 Her particular method of rebellion: Lovell, *Sisters*, 78.

320 As it turned out, her diagnosis was accurate: Lovell, *Sisters*, 95.

321 Like Nancy, she felt she was denied a proper education: Jessica Mitford, *Hons and Rebels*, (London: Phoenix Press of Orion Books, 1999), 92.

322 In 1929 she set up a "Running Away" account: Lovell, *Sisters*, 105.

323 Jessica avidly read about hunger marches: Lovell, *Sisters*, 117.

324 Jessica was deeply influenced by Beverly Nichols' *Cry Havoc*: Lovell, *Sisters*, 119.

325 She was also angered her father's defense of the House of Lords: Jessica Mitford, *Hons and Rebels* (London: Phoenix Press of Orion Books, 1999), 125

326 She may have teased David with the nickname: Jessica Mitford, *Hons*, 39.

327 She spent a year in Paris: Lovell, *Sisters*, 165.

328 While in Europe she allowed Unity to introduce her: Lovell, *Sisters*, 177.

329 By 1935 when she was presented: Lovell, *Sisters*, 178.

330 "Ballroom Communist": Jessica Mitford, *Hons*, 77.

331 Not surprisingly, Jessica became enchanted: Lovell, *Sisters*, 179.

332 Mary Churchill Soames said that her cousins Giles and Esmond Romilly: Mary Soames, *A Daughter's Tale: The Memoir of Winston Churchill's Youngest Child*, (New York: Random House, 2011), 58.

333 It was probably coincidence: Soames, *Daughter's Tale*, 62-63.

334 When news of her actions reached David: Lovell, *Sisters*, 223.

335 "'Whenever I see the words "Peer's Daughter"'": Jessica Mitford, *Hons*, 10.

336 Diana and Unity were already: Lovell, *Sisters*, 229.

337 Young Mary Churchill, though she scarcely knew her cousin Jessica: Soames, *Daughter's Tale*, 94.

338 Jessica and Romilly did consent to marry: Lovell, *Sisters*, 237.

339 It was a measure of Jessica's privileged naiveté: Jessica Mitford, *Hons*, 176.

340 At one point she and Romilly stole: Lovell, *Sisters*, 279.

341 She also experienced some early disillusionment: Lovell, *Sisters*, 255.

342 In such circumstances: Lovell, *Sisters*, 271.

343 Ironically, it was the letters of introductions: Lovell, *Sisters*, 281.

344 Virginia Durr, a wealthy civil rights advocate: Lovell, *Sisters*, 283, 337.

345 Finessing their commitment: Lovell, *Sisters*, 314.

346 They moved to Swinbrook House: Lovell, *Sisters*, 78.

347 Swinbrook House became a beloved home for Deborah: Lovell, *Sisters*, 88.

348 Her athleticism was natural: Lovell, *Sisters*, 114.

349 Dora Carrington, Lytton Strachey's lover: Lovell, *Sisters*, 126.

350 Despite the seeming economic stresses: Lovell, *Sisters*, 241.

351 She, too, met Hitler: Lovell, *Sisters*, 243.

352 Esmond believed that Jessica should have had half: Jessica Mitford, *Hons*, 147.

353 To avoid the notoriety caused by Jessica's elopement: Lovell, Sisters, 238.

354 Political pressures increased when in 1937: Cowles, *Churchill*, 305.

355 On the afternoon of Sunday, September 3, 1939: Lovell, *Sisters*, 297.

Chapter 13

356 "We may fail": Harold Nicolson, *Diaries and Letters, 1930-1939*, (New York: Atheneum, 1967), 104.

357 "I'm very glad to be here": Lynne Olson, *Citizens of London: The Americans Who Stood With Britain In Its Darkest, Finest Hour*, (New York: Random House, 2010), 5.

358 "'It was a terrible war, but if you were the right age'": Olson, *Citizens*, 239.

359 Everyone watched as Ambassador Kennedy advised: Olson, *Citizens*, 37.

360 ""It just isn't possible for me to go off and enjoy my'": Olson, *Citizens*, 41.

361 Where most men would be daunted: Cowles, *Churchill*, 316.

362 An unsympathetic observer might have argued: Cowles, *Churchill*, 318.

363 Although Churchill reminded his countrymen: Cowles, *Churchill*, 359.

364 Churchill also threw his powers of persuasion: Olson, *Citizens*, 7.

365 They joked about "Lord Haw-Haw": Cowles, *Churchill*, 275.

366 Lady Reading led the Women's Voluntary Service: Olson, *Citizens*, 82.

367 Even so, the wealthy began prudently to haul paintings: Smith, *Reflected*, 54.

368 As the months progressed: Smith, *Reflected*, 54.

369 Mary Welsh, *Time-Life* correspondent: Olson, *Citizens*, 100.

370 As Harrison Salisbury put it, "'sex hung in the air like a fog'": Olson, *Citizens*, 388.

371 After the American forces arrived in 1942: Olson, *Citizens*, 241.

372 Virginia Cowles — the American journalist: Cowles, *Looking*, 420.

373 To avoid giving bombers flight reference points: Olson, *Citizens*, 38.

374 There were fines for "lighting": Bryson, *At Home*, 131.

375 Iron railings were removed: Smith, *Reflected*, 70.

376 Churches could no longer ring their bells: Smith, *Reflected*, 70.

377 The imagery of an imminent attack: Smith, *Reflected*, 69.

378 Cowles reported, "Even though the army slept with its boots on": Cowles, *Looking*, 431.

379 Cowles reported that warehouses "made the greatest blaze": Cowles, *Looking*, 414-415.

380 Edward R. Murrow, Edward R. Murrow broadcast of September 8, 1940, University of Kansas, School of Journalism & Mass Communication, http://history.journalism.ku.edu/1940/multimedia/audio/Murrow_broadcasts/wwii_radio.shtml. Accessed May 24, 2019.

381 Ten Downing Street and Buckingham Palace: Olson, *Citizens*, 43.

382 Each morning Londoners picked their way: Smith, *Reflected*, 71.

383 He described the "unsung heroes": Olson, *Citizens*, 46.

384 Reporter Ben Robertson reported: Olson, *Citizens*, 47.

385 Bombed-out buildings in London has large signs: Soames, *Daughter's Tale*, 173.

386 Cowles, covering a bombing raid on Dover: Cowles, *Looking*, 430.

387 Guests at exclusive hotels such as Claridges: Cowles, *Looking*, 421.

388 Lady Camrose refused: Cowles, *Looking*, 420.

389 By March 1941 "Dowagers unable to sleep": Smith, *Reflected*, 77.

390 The level of privation: Smith, *Reflected*, 78.

391 Cowles reported: Smith, *Reflected*, 69.

392 The Savoy Hotel "boasted": Olson, *Citizens*, 45.

393 "He held forth, cocktail in hand": Olson, *Citizens*, 45.

394 Both Churchill's residence at 10 Downing Street and Buckingham Palace: Olson, *Citizens*, 78-79.

395   Over 1,400 civilians died: Smith, *Reflected*, 88.

396   In what were called the Baedeker raids: Sarah Churchill, *Dancing*, 93.

Chapter 14

397   What surprised me most about these gatherings: Cowles, *Looking*, 103.

398   "Everyone seemed determined": Cowles, *Looking*, 243.

399   Hitler had taken Prague on March 15, 1939: Soames, *Clementine*, 115.

400   Tiny and pretty, Diana: Sarah Churchill, *Dancing*, 35.

401   Like other young nobles: Jonathan Guinness, *The House of Mitford*, (London: Phoenix, 1984), 283.

402   Then, in helping her brother Randolph: Sarah Churchill, *Dancing*, 37.

403   She suffered several breakdowns: Sarah Churchill, *Dancing*, 317.

404   At age eight he was sent to boarding school: Winston S. Churchill, *His Father's Son: The Life of Randolph Churchill*, (London: Weidenfeld & Nicolson, 1996; 2004), 43.

405   He was "handicapped by his obsession": Winston S. Churchill, *Son*, 45.

406   Diana Mitford judged "It would have been better": Smith, *Reflected*, 55.

407   Randolph's youngest sister Mary: Olson, *Citizens*, 99.

408   Randolph's erstwhile friend Evelyn Waugh once quipped: Mary S. Lovell, *The Churchills: In Love and War*, (New York: W. W. Norton Company, 2011), 536.

409   He then drew on his family connections: Winston S. Churchill, *Son*, 54.

410   Regardless of his income: Winston S. Churchill, *Son*, 104.

411   His cousin Nancy Mitford wryly commented: Smith, *Reflected*, 58.

412   That future wife: Smith, *Reflected*, 60.

413   They married in October 1939: Winston S. Churchill, *Son*, 173.

414   After this familial relief: Winston S. Churchill, *Son*, 194.

415   Once he boasted to American diplomat Averell Harriman: Winston S. Churchill, *Son*, 493.

416   She traveled to Munich: Smith, *Reflected*, 36.

417   Like other young debutantes: Smith, *Reflected*, 43.

418   Pamela had met Harriman in April 1941: Olson, *Citizens*, 101.

419   Even during times of strict rationing of food: Olson, *Citizens*, 239.

420   He paid for an apartment for her: Smith, *Reflected*, 108.

421   When Harriman was reassigned: Olson, *Citizens*, 244.

422   They may well have been at the Paris Ritz: Olson, *Citizens*, 344.

423   Janet Murrow had borne a son: Smith, *Reflected*, 126.

424   From this point onward: Smith, *Reflected*, 124.

425   Pamela discretely renewed her relationships: Olson, *Citizens*, 390.

426   After Harriman's death in 1986: Olson, *Citizens*, 390.

427   Like her Mitford cousins: Olson, *Citizens*, 110.

428   Similar to Jessica Mitford: Olson, *Citizens*, 112.

429   The couple married On December 24, 1936: Sarah Churchill, *Dancing*, 83.

430 Sarah turned to her father: Sarah Churchill, *Dancing*, 98.
431 A free spirit, she often traveled: Soames, *Daughter's Tale*, 218.
432 Later in the war: Sarah Churchill, *Dancing*, 113.
433 The handsome Winant: Olson, *Citizens*, 104.
434 Though he could have had luxurious food: Olson, *Citizens*, 72.
435 Yet even Sarah's younger sister: Soames, *Daughter's Tale*, 171.
436 Londoners mourned Winant: Olson, *Citizens*, 375.
437 Sarah starred in *The Philadelphia Story*: Sarah Churchill, *Dancing*, 218.
438 Though her parents had never met Beauchamp: Sarah Churchill, *Dancing*, 183-184.
439 Her parents heard about the marriage: Soames, *Clementine*, 550.
440 By 1961 she had accumulated probationary rulings: Sarah Churchill, *Dancing*, 283.
441 In April 1962, they married in Gibraltar: Sarah Churchill, *Dancing*, 301.
442 Sarah died in London in September 1982: Olson, *Citizens*, 386.
443 Her memoirs tell of homey stories: Soames, *Daughter's Tale*, 59.
444 Her sister Sarah was near in age and affection: Soames, *Daughter's Tale*, 47.
445 In a time-honoured ceremony: Soames, *Daughter's Tale*, 137.
446 Even as late as May 1940 during the war: Soames, *Daughter's Tale*, 140.
447 So I waited: Soames, *Daughter's Tale*, 138.
448 About the Blitz Mary recalled, "Whatever terrible things": Emma Soames, "Mary Churchill: The Secret Life of Winston Churchill's Daughter," *The Telegraph* online, 31 October 2011, https://www.telegraph.co.uk/culture/books/8858648/Mary-Churchill-the-secret-life-of-Winston-Churchills-daughter.html. Accessed June 3, 2019.
449 Her mother had to chastise her: Soames, *Daughter's Tale*, 209-210.
450 Initially she found it difficult being the Prime Minister's daughter in the Army: Emma Soames, "Mary Churchill: The Secret Life," 31 October 2011.
451 For the rest of her life: Soames, *Daughter's Tale*, 271.
452 The nearly 850,000 Allied troops: Smith, *Reflected*, 123.
453 As one Briton told Virginia Cowles: Cowles, *Churchill*, 355.
454 Clementine, seeking to sooth her husband: Winston S. Churchill, *Son*, 273.
455 At a time when Parliament ended: Cannadine, *Decline*, 679. This funding change forced the 8th Earl Nelson to sell his Wiltshire house and estate.
456 Friends helped Churchill: Cannadine, *Decline*, 680.

Chapter 15

457 What bedeviled both parents was: Lovell, *Sisters*, 59.
458 He died there in 1958: Lovell, *Sisters*, 454.
459 Sydney survived him: Lovell, *Sisters*, 475.
460 Her husband Paul's open infidelities: Hilton, *Horror*, 132.
461 Her income from writing dwindled: Lovell, *Sisters*, 353.
462 Inspired, she wrote: Lovell, *Sisters*, 357.

463 Her friends included Lady Diana Manners: Hilton, *Horror*, 163.

464 Her continuing publication successes: Hilton, *Horror*, 186.

465 The only spoiling element: Lovell, *Sisters*, 426.

466 In the 1970s she was diagnosed: Lovell, *Sisters*, 486.

467 Pamela became good friends with her ex-husband: Charlotte Mosley, *Letters*, 748-749.

468 One well-loved story: Charlotte Mosley, *Letters*, 659.

469 She seemed to be recovering: Charlotte Mosley, *Letters*, 742-743.

470 When war finally came: Lovell, *Sisters*, 354.

471 A bullet to the spine caused paralysis: Lovell, *Sisters*, 392.

472 Under Regulation 18B: Hilton, *Horror*, 98.

473 With the support of sister Nancy's denunciation: Lovell, *Sisters*, 359.

474 When Diana's cousin Winston Churchill: Lovell, *Sisters*, 349.

475 She demanded that Churchill: Lovell, *Sisters*, 374-375.

476 In fact, this couple, who had not been charged: Lovell, *Sisters*, 362.

477 Still, Winston's wife Clementine: Lovell, *Sisters*, 377.

478 Winston Churchill readily effected a change: Lovell, *Sisters*, 363.

479 Public protests against Churchill's actions: Lovell, *Sisters*, 364.

480 Oswald Mosley still had great private wealth: Lovell, *Sisters*, 457.

481 Their final home: Lovell, *Sisters*, 459.

482 Diana never learned the depths: Lovell, *Sisters*, 325, 328.

483 For some time she remained in a coma: Lovell, *Sisters*, 299.

484 Still, Unity's treatment and recovery: Lovell, *Sisters*, 299.

485 The press coverage: Lovell, *Sisters*, 309.

486 Dependent and limited: Lovell, *Sisters*, 412.

487 They sold their stake in the restaurant: Lovell, *Sisters*, 318.

488 On November 30, 1941: Lovell, *Sisters*, 345.

489 Now 25 years of age: Lovell, *Sisters*, 365.

490 They married: Lovell, *Sisters*, 373.

491 In 1944 Jessica became an American citizen: Lovell, *Sisters*, 376.

492 She literally hid from authorities: Lovell, *Sisters*, 431.

493 By 1956 the revelations: Lovell, *Sisters*, 447.

494 At great personal risk: Lovell, *Sisters*, 429.

495 The book was *The American Way of Death*: Lovell, *Sisters*, 477.

496 She remained a firebrand: Lovell, *Sisters*, 514.

497 When her father David died: Lovell, *Sisters*, 403.

498 When Deborah attempted to smooth the waters: Charlotte Mosley, *Letters*, 626-629.

499 She did visit Chatsworth: Lovell, *Sisters*, 477.

500 Throughout her painful struggle with disease: Lovell, *Sisters*, 523.

501 Even the Queen prepared to do her bit: Nicolson, *Diaries*, 100.

502 Deborah had a wedding gown: Deborah Mitford Devonshire, *Wait For Me*,

(New York: Farrar, Straus, and Giroux, 2010), 113-114.

503 Andrew's uncle Charlie Cavendish was married to Adele Astaire: Deborah Mitford Devonshire, *Memories of Andrew Devonshire*, (Ashbourne, Derbyshire, Horizon Editions Ltd., 2007), 84.

504 After a lengthy courtship: Lovell, *Sisters*, 334.

505 Barely four months later: Devonshire, *Memories*, 24.

506 Among her friends: Smith, *Reflected*, 128.

507 In May of that year Pamela Churchill: Smith, *Reflected*, 146.

508 Midway in their flight: Smith, *Reflected*, 146.

509 Kathleen Cavendish was buried: Lovell, *Sisters*, 410.

Chapter 16

510 If the 10th Duke could have: Lovell, *Sisters*, 421.

511 His death just fourteen weeks short: Lovell, *Sisters*, 423.

512 The tax bill was set at the full rate: Devonshire, *Memories*, 26.

513 The reason for this astronomical debt: Devonshire, *Memories*, 30.

514 In addition, the interest: Devonshire, *Memories*, 26.

515 Chatsworth alone had one and a half acres of roof: Devonshire, *Chickens*, 28.

516 Embracing the industrial innovations of his age: Bryson, *At Home*, 13.

517 The Duke was so enthralled: John Large, "Joseph Paxton: The destitute lad who became the designer of the Grounds of Chatsworth," (Spilsby, Lincolnshire: John Large, 208), 8.

518 Along with John Marples: Large, "Joseph Paxton," 6.

519 The conservatory itself: Large, "Joseph Paxton," 12.

520 During World War II Penrhos College: Devonshire, *Memories*, 34.

521 To do so they sold: Lovell, *Sisters*, 441.

522 She developed "Duchess of Devonshire": Charlotte Mosley, Letters, 718.

523 In addition, the Devonshires: Lovell, *Sisters*, 527.

524 Yet, despite these vigorous efforts: Lovell, *Sisters*, 442.

525 In October 1980 a traveling "Treasures of Chatsworth" exhibit: Charlotte Mosley, *Letters*, 666.

526 By 1998 over five million visitors: Devonshire, *Memories*, 104.

527 Chatsworth estate still covers about 35,000 acres: Cannadine, *Decline*, 688.

528 Other royal visitors to Chatsworth: Devonshire, *Memories*, 43.

529 In 1965 when their son, Peregrine: Cannadine, *Decline*, 687.

530 In August 1990 when their grandson, Lord Burlington: Charlotte Mosley, *Letters*, 726-728.

531 When they celebrated their Golden Anniversary in 1991: Lovell, *Sisters*, 515.

532 In 1994 for the tercentenary: Devonshire, *Memories*, 90.

533 In July 2000, to mark their fiftieth year: Devonshire, *Memories*, 93.

534 Andrew became a member: Cannadine, *Decline*, 666.

535 A measure of Andrew's playfulness: Devonshire, *Memories*, 41.

Chapter 17

536 In 1959, the Westminsters: Cannadine, *Decline*, 650.
537 The Coal Board bought Himely Hall: Cannadine, *Decline*, 643.
538 Lord Montague turned Beaulieu: Cannadine, *Decline*, 646.
539 Baliffscourt, built for the Honorable Walter Guinness: Aslet, *Country Houses*, 311.
540 Utterly unable to maintain the facilities: Cannadine, *Decline*, 644.
541 Aston Clinton was torn down: Bryson, *At Home*, 526.
542 On one hand, it was argued: Cannadine, *Decline*, 637.
543 In 1951 Carlos de Bestegui gave a lavish ball: Hilton, *Horror*, 190.
544 Churchill's 1945 cabinet: Cannadine, *Decline*, Appendix B, 711-712.
545 Further, by 1956: Cannadine, *Decline*, 642.
546 In the ten years "between 1947 and 1957": Cannadine, *Decline*, 645.
547 In 1877 William Morris established a Society: Aslet, *Country Houses*, 14.
548 *Country Life* magazine (established 1897): Aslet, *Country Houses*, 37.
549 Ironically, the magazine: Aslet, *Country Houses*, 42.
550 In this view, the upper class: Cannadine, *Decline*, 639.
551 The public and government were persuaded. English Heritage, "Listed Buildings."
552 In 1950 the palace and grounds were reopened: Cannadine, *Decline*, 647.

Epilogue

553 "Titles are meaningless": Tim Walker, "Aristocrats dismiss the despondent Duke of Devonshire's fears," *The Telegraph*, https://www.telegraph.co.uk/news/politics/7294059/Aristocrats-dismiss-the-despondent- Duke-of-Devonshires-fears.html, 22 February 2010. Accessed May 24, 2019.
554 Her son the 12th Duke of Devonshire: Fay Schlesinger:" 'Aristocracy is dead', says Duke of Devonshire as he offers to surrender his title.," *Dailymail*, https://www.dailymail.co.uk/news/article-1252684/Aristocracy-dead-says-Duke-Devonshire-offers-surrender-title.html, February 2010. Accessed May 24, 2019.
555 At one point he said" Julia Llewellyn Smith: "The Duke of Devonshire: a reluctant reality TV star," *The Telegraph*, https://www.telegraph.co.uk/news/features/9247831/Why-the-Duke-of-Devonshire-is-a-reluctant-reality-TV-star.html, 6 May 2012. Accessed May 24, 2019.
556 When asked how she will cope: Radhika Sanghani, "Meet Lady Burlington, the future Duchess walking in the footsteps of a Mitford," *The Telegraph*, https://www.telegraph.co.uk/women/life/meet-lady-burlington-future-duchess-walking-footsteps-mitford, 21 August 2017. Accessed June 3, 2019.
557 A friend of Prince William: Lianna Brinded, "The Duke of Westminster's death makes Hugh Grosvenor the richest young person in Britain, *Business Insider*, https://www.businessinsider.com/duke-of-westminster-dies-hugh-grosvenor-to-

become-richest-young-person-in-uk-2016-8, 10 August 2016. Accessed June 3, 2019.

558 Soames's mother Catherine: "Who are the Glosse Posse? A look at Britain's most exclusive friendship circle," *Hello Magazine*, https://ca.hellomagazine. com/celebrities/02014100110153/who-are-the-glosse-posse-a-look-at-britain-s-most-exclusive-friendship-circle, 7 August 2018. Accessed June 3, 2019.

559 Even Randolph Churchill's 14-year-old granddaughter: Richard Savill, "Churchill great granddaughter joins march," *The Telegraph*, https://www. telegraph.co.uk/news/uknews/1425311/Churchill-great-granddaughter-joins-march.htmlonline, 22 March 2003. Accessed August 21, 2018.

560 Randolph Churchill's daughter Arabella: "Winston Churchill granddaughter dies great-grandson jailed for drugs," *The Australian*, https://www.theaustralian. com.au/news/world/churchills-rocked-by-death-and-jail/news-story/ ee7a8f685023e49255aab1d6745fece3online, 21 December 2007. Accessed May 29, 2018.

561 In press coverage: Jonathan Beale, "Afghan interpreters petition delivered to Cameron," https://www.bbc.com/news/uk-23684980, 14 August 2013. Accessed August 21, 2018.

562 Winston's great grandson Randolph: Ethan Safran, "Churchill relatives to visit Appleton," *USA Today* Network-Wisconsin, https://www.postcrescent.com/ story/news/local/2017/05/10/churchill-relatives-visit-appleton/101424014/, 10 May 2017. Accessed August 21, 2018.

563 Jonathan Sandys, Diana Churchill's grandson: Paul Grondahl, "Winston Churchill's great-grandson to speak in Albany," *Times Union*, https://www. timesunion.com/local/article/Winston-Churchill-s-great-grandson-to-speak-in-6560012.phponline, 8 October 2015. Accessed August 21, 2018; Cary Darling, "Churchill's Houston descendant sheds light on why he still resonates," *Houston Chronicle.com*, https://www.houstonchronicle.com/life/ article/Churchill-s-Houston-descendant-sheds-light-on-why-12416039.php, 8 December 2017. Accessed August 21, 2018.

564 His preference was for: Cary Darling, "Churchill's Houston descendant," 8 December 2017.

565 This painting of Marrakesh: Joe Warmington, "Winston Churchill 'prolific' painter: great-grandson," *Toronto Sun*, https://torontosun.com/2017/05/13/ winston-churchill-prolific-painter-great-grandson/wcm/454c526f-ca36-4308-b92b-01c1a74ba89aonline, 13 May 2017. Accessed August 21, 2018.

566 On one hand, Diana Mitford's great-granddaughter: Britt Collins, "Interview: Jasmine Guinness," *Guardian*, https://www.theguardian.com/lifeandstyle/2009/ jan/03/interview-jasmine-guinness-ancestry, 2 January 2009. Accessed June 3, 2019.

567 Diana Mitford's granddaughter Daphne Guinness: Rebecca Mead, "Precarious Beauty," *The New Yorker*, https://www.newyorker.com/magazine/2011/09/26/

precarious-beauty, September 26, 2011. Accessed June 3, 2019.

568 However, in March 2008, the *News of The World*: Carole Cadalladr, "Maz Mosley… Me, my mother, Hitler and S&M," *The Independent*, https://www.independent.ie/life/maz-mosley-me-my-mother-hitler-and-sm-31357362.html, 13 July 2015. Accessed May 29, 2018.

569 When his brilliant 39-year-old publicity-shy son Alexander died: Cresseda Connolly, "What happened to the children of Oswald Mosley's Blackshirt followers?," *The Telegraph*, https://www.telegraph.co.uk/books/authors/happened-children-oswald-mosleys-blackshirt-followers/, 2 June 2018. Accessed June 3, 2019.

570 In the 1990s he used his trade: Jonathan Glancey, *"Don't shoot the piano tuner, he's only gone to Cuba,"* *The Independent*, https://www.independent.co.uk/voices/dont-shoot-the-piano-tuner-hes-only-gone-to-cuba-1270404.html, 1 March 1997. Accessed June 3, 2019.

571 In 2014, he challenged the city council: Darren Boyle, "Son of one of the Mitford sisters found to be living in a tent on a beach in Edinburgh in a stand-off with the authorities over a piano he insists on playing," *The Daily Mail*, https://www.dailymail.co.uk/news/article-2607885/Son-one-Mitford-sisters-living-tent-beach-Edinburgh-stand-authorities-piano-insists-playing.html, 18 April 2014. Accessed June 3, 2019.

572 The world in which the 10th Duke of Marlborough: Bryson, *At Home*, 111-112.

BIBLIOGRAPHY

Acton, Harold. *Nancy Mitford: A Memoir*. New York: Harper & Row, 1975.

Aslet, Clive. *The Last Country Houses*. New Haven and London: Yale University Press, 1982.

Bailey, Catherine. *The Secret Rooms: A True Story of A Haunted Castle, A Plotting Duchess, & A Family Secret*. New York: Penguin Books, 2012.

Brendon, Piers. *The Decline and Fall of the British Empire, 1781-1997*. New York: Alfred A. Knopf, 2008.

Bryan, J. and Murphy, Charles J. V. *The Windsor Story*. New York: William Morrow & Company, Inc., 1979.

Bryson, Bill. *At Home: A Short History of Private Life*. New York: Anchor Books, 2010.

Cannadine, David. *The Decline and Fall of the British Aristocracy*. New York: Vintage Books, 1999.

Cannadine, David. *The Rise & Fall of Class in Britain*. New York: Columbia University Press, 1999.

Catherwood, Christopher. *His Finest Hour: A Biography of Winston Churchill*. New York: Skyhorse Publishing, 2010.

Catherwood, Christopher. *Winston Churchill: The Flawed Genius of World War II*. New York: Berkley Caliber, 2009.

Churchill, Sarah. Ed. Paul Medlicott. *Sarah Churchill: Keep on Dancing*. New York: Coward, McCann & Geoghegan, 1981.

Churchill, Winston S. *His Father's Son: The Life of Randolph Churchill*. London: Weidenfeld & Nicolson, 1996.

Clark, Christopher. *The Sleepwalkers: How Europe Went To War in 1914*. New York: Harper Collins, 2013.

The Countess of Carnarvon. *Lady Almina and The Real Downton Abbey: The Lost Legacy of Highclere Castle*. New York: Broadway Paperbacks, 2011.

Courcy, Anne De. *Diana Mosley: Mitford Beauty, British Fascist, Hitler's Angel*. New

York: HarperCollins, 2003.

Courcy, Anne De. *1939: The Last Season*. London: Phoenix, 1989.

Cowles, Virginia. *Looking For Trouble*. New York and London: Harper & Brothers, 1941.

Cowles, Virginia. *Winston Churchill: The Era and the Man*. New York: Harper & Brothers Publishers, 1953.

Cripps-Day, F. H. "The St. Donat's Castle Armoury." *Country Life*. April 2, 1925.

Devonshire, Deborah Mitford. *Memories of Andrew Devonshire*. Ashbourne, Derbyshire: Horizon Editions Ltd., 2007.

Devonshire, Deborah Mitford. *Counting My Chickens and Other Home Thoughts*. New York: Farrar, Straus and Giroux, 2001.

Eksteins, Modris. *Rites of Spring: The Great War and the Birth of the Modern Age*. New York: Anchor Books, 1989.

Fitzgerald, F. Scott. "The Rich Boy." *Redbook*. 1925.

Freedman, Russell. *The War to End All Wars: World War I*. New York: Clarion, 2010.

Greaves, Simon. *The Country House at War: Fighting the Great War at Home and in the Trenches*. London: National Trust Books, 2014.

Gryse, Piet De and Christine Van Everbroeck, eds. *1914-1918: The Great War*. Vlaanderen: Royal Army Museum and Openbaar Kunstbezit, 2007.

Guinness, Jonathan. *The House of Mitford*. London: Phoenix, 1984; 2004.

Hastings, Max. *Catastrophe 1914: Europe Goes To War*. New York: Alfred A. Knopf, 2013.

Hilton, Lisa. *The Horror of Love: Nancy Mitford and Gaston Palewski in Paris and London*. New York and London: Pegasus Books, 2011.

Hochschild, Adam. *To End All Wars: A Story of Loyalty and Rebellion, 1914-1918*. Boston: Houghton Mifflin Harcourt, 2011.

Jackson, Ashley. *Churchill*. New York: Quercus, 2011.

Johnson, Boris. *The Churchill Factor: How One Man Made History*. New York: Riverhead Books, 2014.

Jullian, Philippe. *Edward and the Edwardians*. New York: The Viking Press, 1967.

Large, John. *"Joseph Paxton: The destitute lad who became the designer of the Grounds of Chatsworth."* Spilsby, Lincolnshire: John Large, 2000.

Larson, Erik. *In The Garden of Beasts: Love, Terror, and an American Family in Hitler's Berlin*. New York: Broadway Paperbacks, 2011.

Levkoff, Mary L. and the Los Angeles County Museum of Art. *Hearst the Collector*. "St. Donat's." New York: Abrams, 2008.

Lovell, Mary S. *The Churchills: In Love and War*. New York: W. W. Norton & Company, 2011.

Lovell, Mary S. *The Sisters: The Saga of the Mitford Family*. New York: W. W. Norton & Company, Inc., 2001.

MacColl, Gail and Carol McD. Wallace. *To Marry an English Lord: Tales of Wealth and Marriage, Sex and Snobbery*. New York: Workman Publishing Company, Inc.,

1989, 2012.

Manchester, William. *The Last Lion: Winston Spencer Churchill, Visions of Glory, 1874-1932.* New York: Little, Brown and Company, 1983.

Martin, Ralph G. *Jennie: The Life of Lady Randolph Churchill, 1854-1895.* Englewood Cliffs, N. J., Prentice-Hall, Inc., 1969.

Martin, Ralph G. *Jennie: The Dramatic Years, 1895-1921.* New York: Prentice Hall Press, 1971.

Martin, Ralph G. *The Woman He Loved.* New York: Simon and Schuster, 1974.

Millard, Candice. Hero of the Empire: *The Boer War, A daring Escape and the Making of Winston Churchill.* New York: Doubleday, 2016.

Mitford, Deborah, Duchess of Devonshire. *Wait for Me!: Memoirs.* New York Farrar, Straus and Giroux, 2010.

Mitford, Jessica. *Hons and Rebels* (1960). London: Phoenix Press of Orion Books, 1999.

Mitford, Nancy. *Christmas Pudding* (1932) and *Pigeon Pie* (1940). New York: Vintage Books of Random House, 2013.

Mitford, Nancy. *Highland Fling* (1931). New York: Vintage Books of Random House, 2013.

Mitford, Nancy. *Love in a Cold Climate* (1949). New York: Vantage Books Of Random House, 2010.

Mitford, Nancy. *The Pursuit of Love* (1945). New York: Vantage Books of Random House, 2010.

Mitford, Nancy. *The Water Beetle.* London: Hamish Hamilton, 1962.

Mitford, Nancy. *Wigs on The Green.* New York: Vintage Books, 1935; 2010.

Mosley, Charlotte, ed. *The Mitfords: Letters Between Six Sisters.* London: Fourth Estate, 2012.

Mosley, Diana. *The Duchess of Windsor.* New York: Stein and Day, 1980.

Mosley, Diana. *A Life of Contrasts: The Autobiography of Diana Mosley* (1977; 2002). London: Gibson Square Books, 2003.

Mosley, Nicholas. *Rules of the Game/Beyond the Pale: Memoirs of Sir Oswald Mosley and Family.* Elmwood Park, Illinois: Dalkey Archive Press, 1991.

Nicolson, Harold. *Diaries and Letters, 1930-1939.* New York: Atheneum, 1966.

Nicolson, Harold. *The War Years, 1939-1945. Volume II of Diaries and Letters.* Ed. Nigel Nicolson. New York: Atheneum, 1967.

Olson, Lynne. *Citizens of London: The Americans Who Stood With Britain In Its Darkest, Finest Hour.* New York: Random House, 2010.

Paterson, Michael. *Private Life in Britain's Stately Homes: Masters and Servants in the Golden Age.* Philadelphia: Running Press Book Publishers, 2012.

Pavord, Anna. *Hidcote Manor Garden.* Swindon, Wiltshire: National Trust Enterprises Ltd., 2004.

Prior, Robin and Trevor Wilson. Passchendaele: The Untold Story. New Haven: Yale University Press, 1996.

Pryce-Jones. *Unity Mitford: An Enquiry into Her Life and the Frivolity of Evil.* New

York: The Dial Press, 1977.

Smith, Sally Bedell. *Elizabeth The Queen: The Life of a Modern Monarch*. New York: Random House, 2012.

Smith, Sally Bedell. *Reflected Glory: The Life of Pamela Churchill Harriman*. New York: Simon & Schuster, 1996.

Soames, Mary. *Clementine Churchill: The Biography of a Marriage*. New York: Paragon House Publishers, 1979.

Soames, Mary. *A Daughter's Tale: The Memoir of Winston Churchill's Youngest Child*. New York: Random House, 2011.

Soames, Mary, ed. *Winston and Clementine: The Personal Letters of the Churchills*. Boston: Houghton Mifflin Company, 1998.

Souhami, Diana. *Mrs. Keppel and Her Daughter*. New York: St. Martin's, 1996.

Steele, Philip. *Encyclopedia of British History*. Great Bardfield, Essex: Miles Kelly Publishing Ltd, 2001.

Taggart, Caroline. *Her Ladyship's Guide To the British Season*. London: National Trust Books, 2013.

Thompson, Laura. *The Six: The Lives of the Mitford Sisters*. New York: St. Martin's Press, 2016.

Tuchman, Barbara. *The Guns of August: The Outbreak of World War I*. New York: The Library of America, 1962, 2012.

Tuchman, Barbara. *The Proud Tower: A Portrait of the World Before the War, 1890-1914*. The Library of America, 1962; 2012.

Warwick, Sarah. *Upstairs and Downstairs*. London: Carlton Publishing Group, 2011.

Weintraub, Stanley. *Silent Night: The Story of the World War I Christmas Truce*. New York: The Free Press, 2001.

Westwell, Ian. *The Complete Illustrated History of World War I*. Wigston, Leicestershire Hermes House: 2011.

Willmott, H. P. *World War I*. New York: DK Publishing, 2003.

Wilson, Mark Wilson: forward by Lynn Forney McMurray. *Julia Morgan: Architect of Beauty*. Utah: Gibbs Smith, 2007.

Wright, William. *Omdurman 1898: Battle Story*. Gloucestershire, U. K.: Spellmount, 2012.

Online References Cited

Beale, Jonathan Beale. "Afghan interpreters petition delivered to Cameron," https://www.bbc.com/news/uk-23684980.14 August 2013. Accessed August 21, 2018.

Bevan, Nathan. "Lydia Hearst is Queen of the Castle," Wales Online. https://www.walesonline.co.uk/news/wales-news/lydia-hearst-queen-castle-21560032 August 2008. Accessed June 10, 2019.

Boyle, Darren. "Son of one of the Mitford sisters found to be living in a tent on a beach in Edinburgh in a stand-off with the authorities over a piano he insists on playing." *The Daily Mail.* https://www.dailymail.co.uk/news/article-2607885/Son-one-Mitford-sisters-living-tent-beach-Edinburgh-stand-authorities-piano-insists-playing.html. 18 April 2014. Accessed June 3, 2019.

Brinded, Lianna. "The Duke of Westminster's death makes Hugh Grosvenor the richest young person in Britain." *Business Insider.* https://www.businessinsider.com/duke-of-westminster-dies-hugh-grosvenor-to-become-richest-young-person-in-uk-2016-8. 10 August 2016. Accessed June 3, 2019.

Cadalladr, Carole. "Maz Mosley… Me, my mother, Hitler and S&M." *The Independent.* https://www.independent.ie/life/maz-mosley-me-my-mother-hitler-and-sm-31357362.html. 13 July 2015. Accessed May 29, 2018.

Collins, Britt. "Interview: Jasmine Guinness," *Guardian*, https://www.theguardian.com/lifeandstyle/2009/jan/03/interview-jasmine-guinness-ancestry, 2 January 2009. Accessed June 3, 2019.

Connolly, Cresseda. "What happened to the children of Oswald Mosley's Blackshirt followers?," *The Telegraph.* https://www.telegraph.co.uk/books/authors/happened-children-oswald-mosleys-blackshirt-followers/. 2 June 2018. Accessed June 3, 2019.

Darling, Cary. "Churchill's Houston descendant sheds light on why he still resonates." Houston Chronicle.com. https://www.houstonchronicle.com/life/article/Churchill-s-Houston-descendant-sheds-light-on-why-12416039.php. 8 December 2017. Accessed August 21, 2018.

Glancey, Jonathan. *"Don't shoot the piano tuner, he's only gone to Cuba."* *The Independent.* https://www.independent.co.uk/voices/dont-shoot-the-piano-tuner-hes-only-gone-to-cuba-1270404.html. 1 March 1997. Accessed June 3, 2019.

Grondahl, Paul. "Winston Churchill's great-grandson to speak in Albany," *Times Union*, https://www.timesunion.com/local/article/Winston-Churchill-s-great-grandson-to-speak-in-6560012.phponline. 8 October 2015. Accessed August 21, 2018.

Machen, Arthur. *The Bowmen and Other Legends of the War.* Centenary New: The First World War, 1914-1918. https://centenarynews.com/article?id=1679. Accessed May 24, 2019.

Mead, Rebecca. "Precarious Beauty." *The New Yorker.* https://www.newyorker.com/magazine/2011/09/26/precarious-beauty. September 26, 2011. Accessed June 3, 2019.

MeasuringWorth.com. https://www.measuringworth.com/calculators/exchange/result_exchange.php

Murrow, Edward R. Edward R. Murrow broadcast of September 8, 1940. University of Kansas, School of Journalism & Mass Communication. http://history.journalism.ku.edu/1940/multimedia/audio/Murrow_broadcasts/wwii_radio.shtml. Accessed May 24, 2019.

Nye, Eric W. *Pounds Sterling to Dollars: Historical Conversion of Currency*. http://www.uwyo.edu/numimage/currency.htm. Accessed September 28, 2019.

Safran, Ethan., "Churchill relatives to visit Appleton." *USA Today* Network-Wisconsin. https://www.postcrescent.com/story/news/local/2017/05/10/churchill-relatives-visit-appleton/101424014/. 10 May 2017. Accessed August 21, 2018.

Sanghani, Radhika. "Meet Lady Burlington, the future Duchess walking in the footsteps of a Mitford." *The Telegraph*. https://www.telegraph.co.uk/women/life/meet-lady-burlington-future-duchess-walking-footsteps-mitford. 21 August 2017. Accessed June 3, 2019.

Savill, Richard. "Churchill great granddaughter joins march." *The Telegraph*. https://www.telegraph.co.uk/news/uknews/1425311/Churchill-great-granddaughter-joins-march.htmlonline, 22 March 2003. Accessed August 21, 2018.

Schlesinger, Fay." 'Aristocracy is dead', says Duke of Devonshire as he offers to surrender his title." *Daily Mail*. https://www.dailymail.co.uk/news/article-1252684/Aristocracy-dead-says-Duke-Devonshire-offers-surrender-title.html. February 2010. Accessed May 24, 2019.

Smith, Julia Llewellyn. "The Duke of Devonshire: a reluctant reality TV star." *The Telegraph*. https://www.telegraph.co.uk/news/features/9247831/Why-the-Duke-of-Devonshire is-a-reluctant-reality-TV-star.html. 6 May 2012. Accessed May 24, 2019.

Soames, Emma. "Mary Churchill: The Secret Life of Winston Churchill's Daughter," *The Telegraph* online, https://www.telegraph.co.uk/culture/books/8858648/Mary-Churchill-the-secret-life-of-Winston-Churchills-daughter.html. 31 October 2011. Accessed June 3, 2019.

"St. Donat's." Stradling.org.uk. Accessed 24 May 2019.

Walker, Tim. "Aristocrats dismiss the despondent Duke of Devonshire's fears," *The Telegraph*. https://www.telegraph.co.uk/news/politics/7294059/Aristocrats-dismiss-the-despondent-Duke-of-Devonshires-fears.html. 22 February 2010. Accessed May 24, 2019.

Warmington, Joe. "Winston Churchill 'prolific' painter: great-grandson." *Toronto Sun*. https://torontosun.com/2017/05/13/winston-churchill-prolific-painter-great-grandson/wcm/454c526f-ca36-4308-b92b-01c1a74ba89aonline. 13 May 2017. Accessed August 21, 2018.

"Who are the Glosse Posse? A look at Britain's most exclusive friendship circle." *Hello Magazine*. https://ca.hellomagazine.com/celebrities/02014100110153/who-are-the-glosse-posse-a-look-at-britain-s-most-exclusive-friendship-circle. 7 August 2018. Accessed June 3, 2019.

"Winston Churchill granddaughter dies great-grandson jailed for drugs. "*The Australian*. https://www.theaustralian.com.au/news/world/churchills-rocked-by-death-and-jail/news-story/ee7a8f685023e49255aab1d6745fece3online. 21 December 2007. Accessed May 29, 2018.

INDEX

U

Upper class 3, 5, 6, 13–17, 24, 25, 26, 29–31, 34, 44–46, 48, 49, 51, 52, 53, 56–58, 60, 62, 63, 66, 74, 75, 78, 80, 81, 84–86, 91, 93, 100, 102–105, 117, 123, 128, 133, 139

V

Vacani, School of 27

Vanbrugh, John 11, 12

Vanderbilt, Consuelo (later Duchess of Marlborough) 16, 34, 75, 105

Vanderbilt, Cornelius 15, 32

Vanderbilt, George Washington 6, 76

W

Watts, James 13

Welles, Orson 3

Wells, H. G. 56

Wentworth Woodhouse 31

Wharton, Edith 6, 15

White feathers 62

Whitman, Walt 6

William the Conqueror 14, 17

Williams, Thomas C. 76

Winant, Gil 96, 103, 110

Windsor, ix, x, 55, 120

Wombell, Marie Boyer 52

World War I 36, 53, 54, 55, 56, 57, 58, 59, 60, 61, 62, 63, 64, 71, 72, 77, 86, 87, 94, 109, 127, 134

Worth, Jean 15, 27, 129

Y

Ypres 59, 60, 65, 71, 72